The Dancing Bees

AN ACCOUNT OF THE LIFE AND
SENSES OF THE HONEY BEE

Karl von Frisch
Translated by Dora Ilse

A HARVEST BOOK
NEW YORK
HARCOURT, BRACE & WORLD, INC.

To the English Reader

Suppose German and English bees were living together in the same hive, and one of the Germans found a lot of nectar: its English companions would easily understand what it had to say about the distance and direction of the find. Human language is not so perfect. So I am indebted to Dr. Dora Ilse for interpreting my book for English readers.

For these readers I can wish nothing better than a knowledge of bees, which will bring its own delights.

Munich, 8 November 1953   K. v. FRISCH

A translation of Karl von Frisch's Aus dem Leben der Bienen.
Fifth, revised, edition published by Springer Verlag
(Berlin-Göttingen-Heidelberg) in 1953.

F.12.69

Printed in the United States of America

Preface

IF we use excessively elaborate apparatus to examine simple natural phenomena Nature herself may escape us. This is what happened some forty-five years ago when a distinguished scientist, studying the colour sense of animals in his laboratory, arrived at the definite and apparently well-established conclusion that bees were colour-blind. It was this occasion which first caused me to embark on a close study of their way of life; for once one got to know, through work in the field, something about the reaction of bees to the brilliant colour of flowers, it was easier to believe that a scientist had come to a false conclusion than that nature had made an absurd mistake. Since that time I have been constantly drawn back to the world of the bees and ever captivated anew. I have to thank them for hours of the purest joy of discovery, parsimoniously granted, I admit, between days and weeks of despair and fruitless effort.

The desire to share with others the joy experienced was the motive for writing this little book. In it the observations of other scientists and earlier generations, the discoveries of my fellow workers, and my own discoveries, stand linked together in a brotherly way without any names being mentioned. Facts alone are of interest to us, not the discoverer.

But are there not more than enough bee books? There is the famous book by Maeterlinck, *The Life of the Bee*, or Bonsels' *Maya: the Adventures of a Bee*, both excellent pieces of natural history observation and a joy to the knowledgeable; but the unscientific reader will find it hard to tell where the observation ends and the poetic fancy begins. Again, anyone who wants facts about the life of bees and not the picture of them painted by the creative imagination can look at the text-books; but these are primarily written for the practised bee-keeper, and burdened with many kinds of detail of little inter-est to the amateur naturalist; and, though lacking the genius of the poet, sometimes not devoid of imaginative invention. There are also solid works of scientific research.

I have tried to give the reader the interesting part of the subject, without the ballast of practical instruction that a handbook must provide, without the comprehensiveness of a learned book and the burden of figures, details and documenta-tion with which such a book must be equipped in order to convince; but at the same time I have been careful not to embroider imaginatively on the facts, which are poetic enough in themselves.

Contents

v

Text Illustrations

Plates

CHAPTER ONE

The Bee Colony

THERE are two ways by which the amateur naturalist may easily get acquainted with honey-bees. He can either walk through an orchard or a field full of flowers on a warm spring or summer's day and watch the bees busy foraging at the blossoms; or, passing a bee-keeper's apiary, he may see them flying in and out of the entrances of their hives. A prosperous bee-keeper may keep a few dozen or even more than a hundred beehives in one apiary. If he is a beginner, or if the district is unsuitable for apiculture, he may have just a few beehives, possibly only one. But what he cannot do is to own less than one "beehive", or one "colony of bees", made up of many thousands of individuals; because there is no smaller unit. A farmer may keep a single cow, a single dog, or even a single hen if he so chooses, but one single bee, kept all by itself, would soon perish. This is not as obvious as it sounds, indeed it is very remarkable. If we study the more distant relatives of our bees, we find that they are not in the habit of living together in such large communities. In the case of butterflies, beetles, and dragonflies, we may observe that the male and the female meet at mating time only, soon to separate again, after which each goes his or her own way. The female deposits her eggs in a place where the young larvae after hatching will be able to find their own food. But she does not rear her young, or even recognize them for that matter. Once the eggs are laid, she pays no more attention to them, and usually she dies before the young are hatched. Why then do the honey bees, of all insects, depend upon one another to such an extent that a single bee cannot live by itself, and what exactly is a "colony of bees"?

Supposing our amateur naturalist has come across an apiary owned by a well-to-do bee-keeper who is willing to sacrifice one of his colonies for the sake of providing information on this point. One evening when all the bees have returned from their flight, he closes the entrance and, after spraying the hive with a narcotic, empties it on to the table before the very eyes of our inquisitive friend, who will be surprised by the discovery that so many inhabitants live in one single beehive. If he takes the trouble actually to count them, and provided the colony selected is a fairly strong one, he will find from forty to seventy thousand bees—that is to say, as many bees live in one colony as there are human inhabitants in a fairly large town. And he will not even have counted the *larvae*; these must be specially considered because they are not so easy to see. For the present we shall deal, therefore, with the adult population only.

At first sight, all adult bees look alike. It is true of each of them that the body is divided into three distinct parts: head, chest or thorax, and abdomen. The *head* has two large eyes, one on either side, a mouth underneath, and two feelers in front (pl. 1b). These feelers, present in all insects, reach simply gigantic dimensions in some species, like the longhorn beetles we used to play with when we were children. The *chest*, or *thorax*, has two pairs of wings at the sides, and three pairs of legs underneath; it is joined to the ringed abdomen by a slender waist.

Looking at them more closely we shall, however, discover differences between the various individuals forming a colony. There is *one* bee among them which is distinguished from the rest of the population by its long and slender abdomen; bee-keepers call it the *Queen* (pl. 1b). It is mainly on her that the fate of the colony rests, for better or for worse. She is the only fully developed female in the "Bee State", and, under normal circumstances, the only bee that lays eggs, thus securing the continuation of the race.

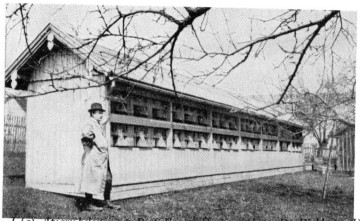

1 (a) *Apiary belonging to Prof. Egerer, Freising (photo: Dr. Wohlgemuth)*

(b) *a, Queen (fully developed female); b, worker bee; c, drone (male bee).* H, *head;* T, *thorax;* A, *abdomen;* E, *eye;* F, *feeler (photo: Dr. Leuenberger, magnification × 2)*

II (a) *An apiary with skeps at a cottage in Uebersee, Upper Bavaria* (*photo: Dr. Wohlgemuth*)

(b) *Straw skep tilted to show combs* (*photo: Prof. Zander*)

(c) *Hollow log serving as hive.* (*photo: Dr. Wohlgemuth*)

Also present, but in larger numbers, are bees of a different type, conspicuous by reason of their thick, plump bodies and their particularly large eyes. These are the male bees or *drones* (pl. 1c) which appear in spring and early summer; later on they become useless and are then forcibly ejected by their fellow bees. We should look for them in vain during the autumn and in winter. All the rest, that is the great majority of the colony, are *worker-bees* (pl. 1b). They are females but do not lay eggs. Thus the very faculty which is so characteristic of their own queen, as well as of the females of most other insects, remains undeveloped in them. On the other hand, the maternal instinct of caring for their progeny, which causes them to feed and nurse the young, is, in these worker bees, developed to an extent unheard of in any other insect; of these duties they completely relieve the queen bee who indeed shows no interest whatsoever in her young. So while the queen bee lays the eggs, it is the worker-bees who look after them. Apart from that, the workers also see to it that the hive is kept clean and at the right temperature; they remove waste matter and dead bees, act as architects of the bee residence, defend the hive if necessary, and busy themselves with the provision of food as well as with its distribution. In short, they perform all the duties with which the queen and the drones do not concern themselves, so that a well-organized division of labour exists among the members of a colony. Indeed this is carried so far that various duties are divided up again among various groups of worker bees, one group having to look after the nursery, another after the food, and yet another after the defence of the hive.

Thus, in a bee colony, the individuals are all interdependent, not one being able to exist by itself alone.

CHAPTER TWO

The Bee's Home

THE bee-keeper places at the disposal of each of his
colonies a wooden box called the beehive, the front of
which is provided with a slit. This is the entrance
through which the bees go in and out. Formerly, bee-keepers
had beehives made of straw, and there are districts where
these straw "skeps" have remained in use to the present
day (pl. IIa).

When, as a child, I was told about the invention of the
telegraph the question which most interested me was, wherever
did the swallows gather for their autumn migration before
there were telegraph wires? Similarly, the reader may ask,
where did the bees live before they were domesticated by
man? However old apiculture may be—and we know from
paintings in their temples and royal tombs that the Egyptians
kept bees as long as five thousand years ago—the bees themselves are certainly older still and must have lived in the open
before man started keeping them.

A colony of bees will sometimes escape from the beekeeper
and settle in a wood in the hollow trunk of a dead tree. This
is the original dwelling of the honey-bees; and as there were
then many more hollow trees than in our own days of improved forest cultivation, no housing problem existed for bees
in ancient times.

Like a straw basket or wooden box, the hollow tree provides
no more than external protection. It is the bees themselves
who, by constructing honeycombs of wax, build the internal
structure of their home (pl. IIb).

4

Some bee-keepers offer as a dwelling a wooden block, which is in fact a piece of hollow tree-trunk (pl. IIc). This type of beehive comes nearest to the original home of the bees. Straw baskets on the other hand, while offering a similarly protected hollow space, are lighter and handier and better for keeping out the cold in winter, and are therefore preferable to the other types. However, neither of these old-fashioned bee-dwellings is very practical, as the bee-keeper cannot easily get at the inside of the hive. Thus, it was a big step forward in apiculture when some decades ago somebody had the bright idea of offering the bees as a living-room a wooden box—the back wall and lid of which could be removed—with a number of hanging wooden frames within which the bees could build their combs (pl. IIIa). Thus, whenever there is anything to examine or to repair inside the hive, each comb can be lifted out separately with its frame and then put back again. Also it is possible to remove each separate framed comb when filled with honey, and to replace it with an empty frame without unduly disturbing the colony. With the old types of hive, extraction of honey meant destruction of the dwelling, and more often than not, annihilation of the whole colony. For this reason, these modern hives with "movable frames" have been widely adopted.

The fact that this type of hive can also be moved bodily constitutes a further great advantage. The original dwelling, the hollow tree, was fixed to a particular spot. Boxes or baskets, on the other hand, can be loaded on to a wagon and moved to other districts by the bee-keeper, if the nectar flow is diminishing in his own district while still promising a rich harvest elsewhere. In many districts of Austria this mobile type of apiculture provides an excellent way of increasing the honey crop. In all those places where, towards the end of the general nectar flow, untold millions of plants full of nectar are still in flower during a few weeks in late summer— that is to say, in extensive fields of buckwheat, or in huge areas of heather—bee-keepers gather from all sides to set up their hives, just as Swiss peasants drive their herds to their

mountainside pastures at certain times of the year in order to
utilize an otherwise unused strip of land.

The bee-keeper provides the hive and the wooden frames
for building the combs; but the combs are built in by the
bees themselves. Even the very substance from which the
combs are built—the *wax*—is produced by them; each worker
bee carries with her a minute wax factory.

All this sounds miraculous, and even the fact that making
wax is no peculiarity of bees alone does not make it any more
credible. Wax-making is found in other insects too. In some
parts of Europe, during summer, for example, tiny white
flecks may be seen sailing through the air like minute snowflakes. After catching such "snowflakes" and examining them
closely, we recognize them as greenflies covered with a fur
made of the finest white threads of wax which have been
exuded through pores in their skin. Bees exude wax from the
underside of their abdomen; its chemical composition resembles that of a fat. As shown in pl. IIIb, small thin scales of
wax appear in the depth of those folds of the skin which are
formed between the abdominal segments. The bees, instead
of allowing these tiny scales to drop and be wasted, remove
them with their feet, and knead them into small wax lumps
with the help of their strong jaws or mandibles—useful tools
which grow at the sides of their mouths (pl. IIIb, M.) From
these lumps, little by little, they build up the honeycomb.

Building does not go on continuously inside the hive, but it
can be done at great speed if necessity arises. The photograph in pl. IVa shows the amount of work carried out during
a single night by these tiny master-builders; and this is by
no means an unusual achievement. The picture shows that
building proceeds from top to bottom.

Each honeycomb consists of several thousands of little
waxen chambers or "cells" serving partly as nurseries for the
young brood, partly as larders for the storage of food. It is
surprising how well they are fitted for their purpose. If we
cut transversely through a comb from top to bottom, we shall
obtain a section as in pl. IVb. The central wall M which, like

III (a) *Bee hive. The lid is off and a frame with its comb has been lifted out. E, entrance hole in front wall of hive. In front of it the alighting board*

(b) *A bee exuding wax, seen from below. W, small scales of wax coming out of folds of skin*

(c) *Front view of head of bee. M, mandibles; T, sucking tongue; F, feeler; E, eye (enlarged)*

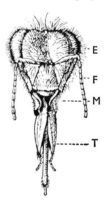

IV (a) Building the comb

(b) The cell structure of the comb, showing left, a downward section, with M the middle wall; and, right, the surface of the comb

M

M

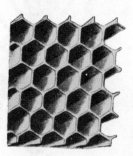

the rest of the comb, is built from wax, forms the common partition or base for the cells extending from it on either side. The floor of each cell is slightly hollowed out, its cavity being fitted in skilfully with that of its opposite number, in such a way as to make the best use of the available space. Each cell has a slight downward tilt towards the centre wall, just sufficient to prevent the viscous honey store from trickling out. Most remarkable of all is the fact that the side walls

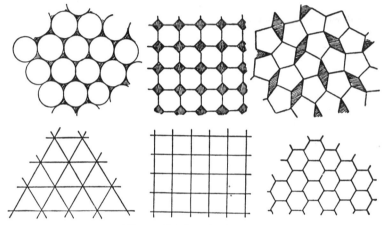

Fig. 1. (*Explanation in text.*)

of each cell combine to form a regular hexagon (pl. ivc). It is true that the bees could just as well build chambers with round walls, as in fact do the bumble-bees; or they could build them with some number of side walls other than six (fig. 1); but, in the case of cylindrical cells, or of cells with say five or eight walls, unused interstices would remain between them (dark hatching in fig. 1, upper row), which would mean waste of space. Moreover, each cell would require walls of its own, either wholly or in part, which would mean waste of valuable material. Both these disadvantages disappear in cells so constructed that their cross-sections form either triangles or squares or hexagons (fig. 1, lower row), for in these geometrical shapes each wall forms also the wall of an adjacent cell, and there are no spaces left between the cells. In fig. 1, lower row, triangles, squares, and hexagons are drawn in such a way as to enclose equal areas. Given the same depth, each cell must therefore contain the same amount of honey. But, as we may easily discover by measurement, the hexagon has the smallest circumference and therefore requires the least amount of building material. Moreover hexagons are much better fitted to receive the roundish larvae which are to be reared in these little chambers, than cells with triangular or square cross-sections could ever be.

The bees, with their hexagonal cells, have in fact discovered the best and most economical plan conceivable. How they arrived at this none of our learned men has so far been able to discover. Their writings and discussions on the subject are many, but they have not yet solved the riddle.

We have already briefly mentioned the twofold purpose of the bees' cells. In them provisions are stored, and they are the cradles of the coming generation. Let us now deal with the origin and nature of the food, and with the bees' brood.

CHAPTER THREE

How Bees Feed

ECCENTRICS with preferences for particular food occur among animals as well as among human beings. But whereas people can indulge a wide range of tastes, animals cannot. Here, nature dictates more strictly to each species what to eat and what to avoid. This is particularly true of insects. We know of a caterpillar, for example, which will not feed on anything but willow leaves, and of these, only on sallow. It would rather starve than feed on the leaves of another willow species, let alone of another plant. There are also caterpillars which can live only on the horns of dead cattle or the antlers of antelope. Some beetles live exclusively on timber, and there are certain fleas that care only for the blood of moles. On the other hand, there are caterpillars which will eat a dozen or so different sorts of leaf, a flea which will suck blood from man, dogs, cats, rats, or even birds, whichever happens to come along, and there are ants which feed on honey, fruit, or meat with equal avidity, wherever they may find it.

These differences are all the more strange since both man and animals, no matter whether omnivorous or specializing in certain foods, require the same essential foodstuffs in order to keep alive; it is only the form in which the foodstuffs are taken that differs in the various cases.

We all need fat and sugar in our diet, as fuel with which to run the machines of our bodies and as a source of energy for moving our muscles, just as urgently as a locomotive needs fuel in order to be able to move and do its own work. To

9

the children be it said that for this purpose we need not eat
sweets all the time. As the main constituent of bread and
potato, called "starch", is not only chemically related to
sugar, but is actually turned into sugar after every meal by
our digestive organs, these two can provide the sugar necessary for our body just as well as sweets. We all need proteins
besides, and these we take in mainly in the form of meat;
though in smaller quantities we get them also from bread,
milk, and a number of other foods. Protein in pure form, or
albumen, occurs abundantly in the white of an egg (the
German for albumen is "eiweiss" or "egg-white"). As the
very substance of the living body, both animal and human,
consists largely of proteins, we can grow only if provided with
proteins in our diet.

Bees also need these two types of food and they are seldom
found in so clearly separated forms as in the two substances
which make up all the food collected and brought home to the
colony by the foraging bee. One of these, the *nectar*, is rich
in sugar but almost free from proteins; it provides the fuel
necessary for the working of the bee's body. The other
substance, the *pollen*, is rich in protein, and supplies the building material indispensable for bodily growth. They are both
found in flowers, and form the foraging bees' sole objective.

In winter, after the flowers have gone, there are still
hungry mouths to be fed. For this reason, during spring and
summer, while the nectar flow is rich, bees collect a surplus
of honey which will see them through the winter. On the
other hand the rearing of the young bees, for whose growing
bodies protein is indispensable, is limited to the spring and
summer season, when plants are in flower. Accordingly, a
surplus of pollen is collected then, and stored not so much as
a provision against the winter, but just so as to guarantee the
feeding of the brood during a long period of summer rain.

What honey is, and how bees collect it

If we pluck a head of clover and, carefully pulling off some
of the separate florets of which it is composed, begin to chew

their tubular ends, we notice a distinctly sweet taste. Provided the bees have not previously robbed the florets too thoroughly we may even see a clear droplet of almost pure sugar solution glistening at the end of each. Most flowers produce this sugary juice at the base of their petals. Botanists call it nectar—not without reason. This was the name given by the ancient Greeks to the drink of the gods. Not only did it have a wonderful scent, but it made men immortal. Honey too has a definite scent and, even if it does not ensure

Fig. 2. Flower of Ruta graveolens. *Droplets of honey are exuded by the annular pad* P *in the middle of the flower.* St, *Stamens (magnified three times).*

immortality, many old bee-keepers—as well as some doctors —are convinced that to eat honey is healthy and prolongs life. How this happens and whether in fact it is correct remains for science to discover.

There is one type of flower in which the nectar droplets are freely exposed at the base of their slightly convex petals (see fig. 2); these have among their visitors, apart from bees, a number of flies, beetles, and sundry other pilfering insects. Another type of flower secretes nectar at the base of its deep petal tubes where it can be found only by insects well equipped for this special task. Examples of these are our native clover and the flower of an exotic plant called Thermopsis (fig. 3). It is the mobile, ingeniously constructed proboscis protruding from the mouths of bees, bumble-bees, and butterflies (pl. 3c) that enables these insects to suck up nectar into their stomachs even from long tubular flowers.

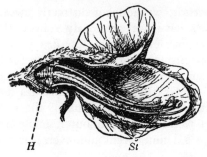

Fig. 3. *Flower of* Thermopsis montana, *longitudinal section. Honey* H *is secreted at the bottom of the deep floral tube.* St, *Stamens (magnified two times).*

Whatever gets into our stomachs is digested, absorbed into our body fluids, and becomes part of us. The bee's stomach, on the other hand, is like a shopping-bag (see fig 4, H); what it contains belongs to the whole family, the whole colony of bees. Whenever a flower is visited, several droplets of nectar are sucked up by the proboscis and reach the honey sac after having passed through the long gullet. As soon as the bee returns from her flight, she brings up the contents of her honey sac which are then transferred to the honey cells and serve as a store. Naturally she uses some of it to feed herself.

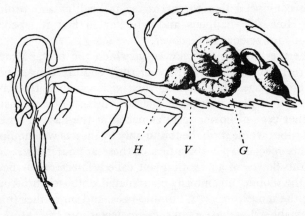

H   V   G

Fig. 4. *Alimentary canal of bee.* H, *honey sac or honey stomach.* G, *gut.* V, *valve separating the two.*

Whenever she feels hungry she just opens the valve connecting the communal stomach with the adjacent gut (V in fig. 4). Only after passing this valve can the honey be digested, and used for the requirements of the individual bee's body.

It is incorrect to say that bees collect honey; they collect nectar, from which they make honey. Freshly collected nectar is distributed amongst the members of the colony who, by means of repeated regurgitations, expose droplets of it to the warm air through their mouths. In this way, much of the water evaporates and the substance then thickens once more in the open cells. Honey, which keeps well, develops out of the thin nectar within a few days. At the same time, by the addition of glandular secretions, sugar is transformed into an easily digestible form by the same process that goes on in our own digestive tracts. The work of digestion is thus performed in advance. Also, by a process still unknown to us, the honey absorbs certain substances from the flowers and also from the bees' bodies which increases its food value. In this way, bees convert the sweet juices of flowers into a delicious food.

But we should not forget that all the sugar is derived from nectar and that the aroma comes only from the scent of the blooms with, in addition, the scent of bees and wax. So in effect the flowers are the creators of honey, though we must thank the bees for improving it—and indeed for its presence on our tables—for no man would have the patience to collect the tiny droplets of nectar.

A drop of honey brought home by one single bee is rather small, her honey-stomach being not much bigger than the head of a pin. In order to collect a thimbleful of honey she would have to fill, empty, and refill it about sixty times. However, the droplet of honey in a single floret is smaller still. Our foraging bee must visit between one thousand and fifteen hundred single florets of clover just to fill her honey-stomach once. The fact that during a favourable season some colonies nevertheless manage to store more than two pounds of honey in a single day goes to show how industrious they must have been. The glutton who swallows honey by the spoonful should sometimes stop to think of the enormous amount of work which must have gone into its production.

Pollen and the bee's pollen basket

Pollen is much more easily detected in a flower than nectar, the droplets of which are often concealed from sight. Pollen is produced in so-called "anthers" which form the upper part of "stamens". These stamens (see figs. 2 and 3, St.), which vary in number according to the species of the plant, grow up from the base of the flower as delicate filaments which broaden into small pads at their free ends. In these pads the pollen is formed, mostly in the form of a yellow or, in some flowers, a whitish-yellow or reddish powder, and often in such quantities that the slightest touch is sufficient to cover our fingers with dust. From these anthers the foraging bees collect their pollen.

As a rule, it is not one and the same group of worker-bees that collect both honey and pollen. In a colony of bees division of labour is arranged as thoroughly as in a boot and shoe factory where a number of hands are employed, each in a different capacity: one for cutting the leather, another for stitching the cut-out parts on a machine, a third for hammering nails in, and so on. Each one by keeping within the strictly limited range of a certain activity acquires a special skill. Something very similar takes place in the bee's workshop: here the various activities are distributed among various groups of bees to such an extent that even the foragers are subdivided into a group of nectar-collectors and one of pollen-collectors, each group devoting itself exclusively to its own particular task. Nor is the collecting of pollen by any means an easy job; even an accomplished juggler may gaze with respect at the skill displayed by the bees in this process.

The bees who collect the pollen do not swallow it as they would nectar, but mould it into a solid mass which is then attached to the outer side of their hind legs. Most of you will

have seen a pollen-collector making for home with her legs
coated with pollen, looking as if she wore plus-fours. (The
German word for these pollen balls is actually *Höschen*, or
breeches.) (See pl. va.) The movements necessary for this
process of collecting are carried out at such an incredible
speed that our eyes can hardly follow them. It requires some
ingenuity to find out exactly what they are.

Good work requires above all things good tools, and with
these the worker-bees have been provided by nature. Plate vb
shows the way in which her legs are attached to her body. A
bee's leg, like every other insect's, consists of several parts
attached to each other by flexible joints. Here we are interested
only in the following most important parts: the thigh or
femur, the shank or tibia, and finally the foot or tarsus, in
itself made up of several segments. The hind legs (see pl. vc)
play an essential part in pollen-collecting; their first tarsal segments, greatly enlarged and broadened as compared with the
rest, are provided on their inner sides with a thick trimming
of stiff bristles called pollen combs. Another peculiarly shaped
part of the hind leg is the tibia; its outside is surrounded by a
fringe of long hairs which enclose between them a smooth
area slightly concave in places. This is the so-called "pollen
basket" in which the pollen loads are carried home. And this
is how they get there.

Every pollen-collecting bee starts by filling her honey sac
with a small amount of honey on her way out of the hive.
Once arrived at a flower—and this can be watched particularly well among the flowers of poppies or wild roses—she
settles on the stamens, nimbly scraping off the loose pollen
with her jaws and front legs, while at the same time moisten-
ing it with the honey brought along for the purpose, so as to
make it sticky. If there is enough pollen it will get stuck
between the hairs of her body while she is working the blossoms, so that at times she looks as if she were dusted all over
with flour. While flying on to the next blossom, she is fever-
ishly moving her legs underneath her body. With the pollen
combs on her hind legs she first scrapes off the pollen from her

coat and from the rest of her legs, next with a sort of curry-comb of stiff bristles situated at the end of her tibia, called the pecten (see pl. vc, 2), she scrapes out the combfuls of pollen in the opposite leg, changing from one side to the other, so that the pollen now hangs in the pecten, but for a short moment only; thereupon a skilful pressing movement from a rammer called the auricle (pl. vc, 2) pushes it through the gap (G) and over to the other, outer, side of the tibia, up into

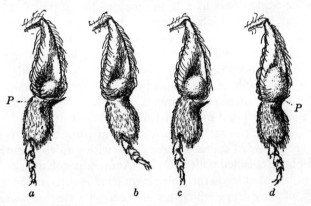

Fig. 5.   *Hindleg of a worker-bee collecting pollen.* (a) *at the beginning,* (d) *towards the end of her foraging flight. The picture shows the gradual enlarge-ment of the "plus-fours". In* (b) *and* (d) *a load of pollen is just being pressed into the basket from below through the action of the pecten* P. (*After Casteel.*)

the basket. In this way one lot after another is pushed up into the basket from below, the "breeches" are growing and are pushed up further and further, until finally in some cases they completely fill up the pollen basket (fig. 5). Every now and then, too, the two middle legs ram and pat each pollen load from the outside so that the mass may stick together and not get lost.

When a bee gets home she slips off her "breeches" and puts them in a waxen cell. Honey and pollen never get mixed together; each of these two foods is stored in a separate group of cells inside the honeycombs, to be taken out again when needed.

*V (a) Pollen collector on
return journey with
full pollen baskets
(photo: Dr. Leuenberger)*

*(b) Honey bee (worker).
A, eye; F, feeler.* × 3½

*(c) Hindleg of a worker bee, seen (1) from the outside, (2) from the inside.
The first tarsal segment, greatly enlarged, carries the pollen comb, C,
on its inner side. Pollen is scraped out of the pollen comb by means of
the pecten, P, on the opposite hindleg. Pressure exerted by the auricle,
A, squeezes the pollen out of the pecten, through the gap, G, towards
the outside of the tibia into the basket, B (a cavity surrounded by a
fringe of hairs), in which the pollen is carried home*

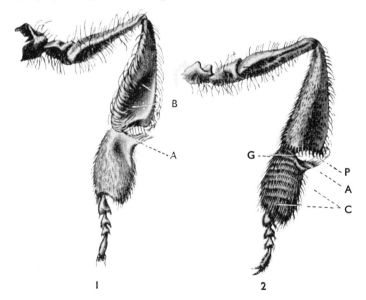

VI (a) *Effect of the visit of bees on the growth of fruit. One of the two pear branches was covered with gauze when in blossom, so that bees could not reach it. Not a single fruit developed from it whereas thirty-three pears grew on the other (after Zander)*

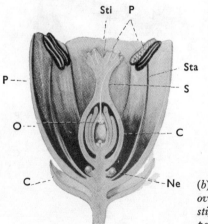

(b) *Longitudinal section of flower.* O, *ovary;* C, *carpel;* S, *Style;* sti, *stigma ;* P, *pollen;* Sta, *stamen,* P, *petal;* C, *colyx,* Ne, *Nectar*

How flowers benefit from being raided by bees

Bees do no harm by collecting honey and pollen from flowers, for the plant also benefits from yielding these two foods.

Pollen grains are the male germ cells of flowering plants, corresponding to the sperm of animals. The female germ cells or ovules, corresponding to the eggs of animals, are often —but not always—produced by the same flower as the pollen. The ovules lie in a swelling of the flower base called the ovary (pl. vib). Just as a hen's egg cannot develop into a chick unless fertilized by the sperm of a cock, so the ovules inside the ovary can turn into ripe seeds, able to germinate and later grow into young plants, only after uniting with male germ cells or sperm.

In order to fertilize the ovary, some of the pollen must reach the sticky stigma; in other words, the flower must be "pollinated" (see pl. vib, St.). From the stigma the contents of the pollen grain travel down the style of the flower (S) and unite with the ovule. There can be no development of seed unless the pollen reaches the stigma. As a rule, the flower, being unable to move, cannot shed pollen from its anthers on to its own stigma; nor would this be desirable—just as with animals strict inbreeding is supposed to be harmful. Healthier progeny is obtained if pollen from one flower reaches another flower of the same plant, and there are various means by which this result is achieved. Frequently flowers are not susceptible to pollen which they themselves have produced, so that self-fertilized flowers remain sterile.

In its flight from poppy to poppy, or from rose to rose, a pollen forager carries pollen from one flower to another. As dusty from her work as a mill-hand, the bee inevitably leaves a few pollen grains on the stigma of the next flower visited, thus pollinating and helping to fertilize it. But even the honey-collectors touch some of the anthers and stigmata as they strive to reach the sweet nectar in the receptacle, and in this way involuntarily act as plant-breeders. With what success may be shown in a picture (pl. vib) more clearly than in words. At blossom-time two branches of a pear tree were selected, each carrying the same amount of blossoms. One of the branches was tied up with gauze so that the bees could not get at it. The branch whose blossom the bees could get at produced thirty-three pears, whereas the other one did not bear a single fruit.

It is true that other insects also act as pollinators; on a fine spring day one can see a mixed crowd of bumble-bees, butter-flies, hawkmoths, beetles, and flies busying themselves among the flowers. Yet the most important carriers of pollen are the honey-bees, because of their great number, their diligence in collecting, not only for their immediate needs, but also for laying up winter stores, and last but not least, their good equip-ment which enables them to exploit flowers that cannot be worked by insects with less perfect tools. If it were not for the bees, not only fruit trees but clover and buckwheat, beans and cucumbers, bilberries and cranberries, and innumerable meadow flowers and other plants would bear far fewer fruit, or none at all. But the fruits of today are the plants of to-morrow; the next generation grows from the seed. Plants that produce few seeds die out. By secreting nectar many flowers attract insects which, while finding honey, also obtain some of the abundant pollen. However, they are not looters; in receiving they also give. They effect pollination, ensuring the growth of the seed and the continuation of the species. A beautiful reciprocity, all the more to be marvelled at as neither of the two partners has the slightest idea of what they are doing.

CHAPTER FOUR

The Brood

A YOUNG chick just hatching from the egg is undeveloped in some respects, but on the whole it resembles its parents, and like these it has legs and wings, eyes and beak, etc. Out of the bee's egg, on the other hand, a little white grub emerges which shows not the slightest resemblance to its mother, having neither head, eyes, wings, nor even legs.

This is the same with other insects. Nobody, looking at those maggots which, to the housewife's horror, sometimes appear in a half-forgotten, smelly piece of meat or in over-ripe cheese, could guess that they would later turn into flies. And if we did not know it from childhood we certainly could never guess that caterpillars become butterflies, so totally different is the appearance of the two.

There is good reason why birds hatch out complete with wings while insects emerge as wingless, worm-like larvae. Insects have no bones in their bodies but have a strong outer armour instead. In the case of larvae this is still relatively fragile, but anyone who has held a beetle in his hand will know how hard it feels. During the process of growth, this shell bursts from time to time, the insect sheds its skin and, within a few hours, grows a little and builds a new shell. This shedding of the skin is no small matter, as the living body inside has to emerge safely out of the suit of armour. The flat, broad wings of a bee or butterfly would present great difficulties in this process. That is why insects have no wings while they are growing, or only short wing-stumps.

When a bee larva or a caterpillar grows it becomes a pupa.

Outwardly this seems a restful stage, but inwardly it is full
of reorganization and development until the pupa too bursts
its shell and the winged insect emerges after the final moult.
The adult cannot grow any more, as it can no longer shed its
skin. It is a fallacy, though a widely held one, that a small
beetle is a young beetle; in reality a young beetle looks like a
yellow grub or a whitish maggot.

To return to our bees: if we look for the queen in a suitable
observation hive, at the right time, we generally find her
occupied in walking slowly, almost majestically, across the
combs to deposit her eggs. During the spring season an efficient queen can lay about fifteen hundred eggs in twenty-four
hours, that is, she lays on the average one egg per minute by
day and by night. Actually she takes periods of rest and lays
correspondingly faster in between. Yet in proportion the bee's
eggs are not so very small: those fifteen hundred eggs laid in
a day have collectively the same weight as the queen herself.
One can see how fast the eggs must grow inside their mother,
and one understands why the queen is not free for any other
occupation.

In depositing her eggs, the queen proceeds as follows:
first she puts her head inside a cell to convince herself that it
is empty, and is also suitable for the reception of an egg (fig. 6).
If this is the case, she then lowers her abdomen into it and
stays absolutely still for a few seconds. When she withdraws
her abdomen we can see the oblong egg standing on the
bottom of the cell, while the queen has already gone off in
search of another cell to lay her next egg.

One must not imagine that in doing this she wanders aimlessly about the combs, depositing one egg here, one there.
This would be a great drawback for the bee-keeper who
would, in this case, have to destroy part of the brood with
every honeycomb he took from the hive. And the purchaser
of such a comb would pull a long face if he found it pervaded
by white maggots. In fact a well-defined order prevails. The
queen deposits her eggs in the front and central combs of the
hive only, and in the central but not in the outer parts of these

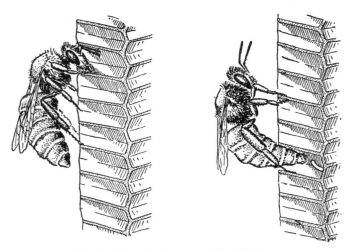

Fig. 6.   *Queen in the process of egg laying.*
Left, *examining a cell to find out its suitability for receiving an egg.*
Right, *depositing an egg in the cell.*

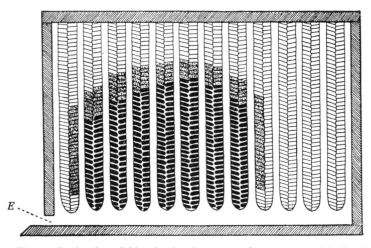

Fig. 7.   *Section through hive showing the extent and arrangement of the brood nest in relation to the combs. black: cells containing brood; dotted: cells containing pollen; white: cells containing honey. E, entrance hole.*

chosen combs. Thus originates the "brood nest" whose
approximate extent at the time of abundant breeding is indicated in the diagram in fig. 7. The cells painted black contain
the eggs and the larvae of the bees. Lifting out such a comb,
we find the lower part filled with brood (pl. VII). In the adjacent cells the worker-bees store the pollen so that the brood
region is usually surrounded by a border of pollen cells
(dotted in fig. 7, marked P in pl. VIIb). Honey is deposited in
the outermost cells of the brood combs, but also in all the
combs behind and in front of the "brood nest" and, in many
hives, on top of it (white cells in fig. 7). The sections entirely
filled with honey are those which the bee-keeper can take
away from the bees at the time of the honey harvest. But he
must not take them all; he must estimate how much he will
have to leave as winter provision for the colony. It is the
excess only that he may use for himself.

After three days a small white larva hatches from the
deposited egg (pl. VIIb). It is at once supplied with food in its

a

b

Fig. 8.

(a) *egg of bee.*
(b) *Larva six
days after
emerging from
egg.*
Magnification
× 2

cell by worker-bees and develops such an appetite
that it completes its whole growth within six
days. Figure 8 shows in exact proportion the
size of a bee's egg and that of a six-day-old larva.
During these six days its weight has increased
more than five-hundred-fold. In human terms
this would mean that a newborn babe had
attained the weight of about a ton and a half.
Now follows a stage of external quiescence
during which the transformation of the larva
into the completed bee is achieved. The worker-
bees now build a slender vaulted lid of wax over
the cell and, as if it wanted to emphasize its need
for complete rest, the larva itself spins a dense
web underneath this cap from the inside, comparable to the cocoon which caterpillars often
make before pupating. The bee-keeper calls this
stage that of the "sealed brood" (pl. VIIa, SB), in contradistinction to the still growing "open brood" (pl. VIIa, OB).

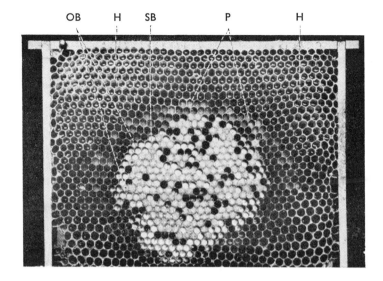

VII (a) Brood comb, OB, *open brood;* SB, *sealed brood;* H, *honey;* P, *pollen*

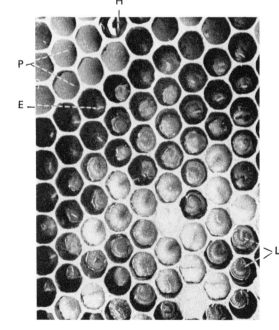

(b) Section of the edge of a brood nest. E, *eggs;* L, *larvae of various ages;* (P), *pollen;* H, *honey (photo:*

Dr. Leuenberger)

(b) Bees emerging

VIII (a) Section through a covered breeding cell showing the dormant pupa within

(c) Section of comb with two queen cells in each of which one queen is being raised

(d) Section of brood comb. Top: cells for the breeding of workers. Below: larger cells for the breeding of drones (photo: Dr. Roesch)

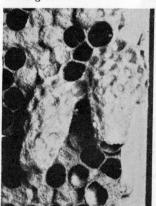

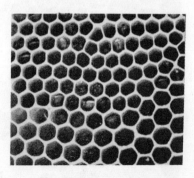

Inside the closed cell the larva turns into a pupa (pl. VIIIa), and on the twelfth day after the beginning of the quiescent phase, exactly three weeks after the egg is laid, the lid or capping is broken, and the complete winged bee climbs out of its cell (pl. VIIIb).

As the queen lays eggs from early spring to late autumn, broods may be found in all stages of development between early March and October. More than a thousand young workers hatch out daily during the summer months. Equally great is the daily death rate of older bees which have reached the end of their life's span or which have met with some accident on one of their collecting flights. The brood cells from which the bees have hatched are soon filled again with eggs by the queen. The nursing of the brood by workers is not confined to the six days of growth during which the larvae must be fed. From the egg stage to the time of hatching out, the brood needs attention, since a regular temperature of 95° F. is necessary for its development. This temperature in the hive is produced and maintained by the workers. Another kind of example will make this clear. The human body maintains a normal temperature of 98·4° F. without variation day and night, summer and winter, and on this all its functions depend. This is only possible through temperature adjustment outside our control and mostly without our knowledge. Should the body temperature rise for only a fraction of a degree above normal, the blood flows more quickly into the skin, making it hotter and causing the face to become flushed. The inner heat is thus lowered and we begin to sweat. Through the evaporation of sweat, heat is used up and the body begins to cool. Should the body temperature fall too much, the external temperature is diminished by different distribution of the blood and more fats and sugar (the heating materials of the body) are burned. When we begin to shiver, this is merely an involuntary muscular reaction set up to produce warmth.

This capacity for regulating body temperature is only found in mammals and birds. A lizard is hot-blooded and full of

energy when the sun is warm, but in the cool of the evening its
blood temperature falls, and it becomes sleepy and lazy. Insects too cannot maintain a constant body temperature but are
quite dependent on the temperature of their surroundings.
This applies to butterflies, beetles, flies, and equally to bees
which, when on foraging flights—dependent on themselves
alone—become stiff and immobile at a temperature of about
50° F. should evening overtake them. The constant temperature of 95° F. maintained in the breeding-cells is achieved
by an astonishing process. Workers crowd together in their
thousands on top of the cells so as to make use of their col-
lective warmth. In cooler weather they crowd together and
cover the brood cells with their bodies, as with an eiderdown.
On warmer days they scatter and, if the heat becomes excessive, they bring in water—as they cannot sweat—and cover
the combs with a fine film which they cause to evaporate by
fanning with their wings. They sit like little living ventilators
over the cells, driving the warm air towards each other and
pushing it out again through the entrance. The explanation
of this wonderful achievement lies of course in an instinctive
sense of the correct temperature which human beings do not
possess to the same extent, coupled with well-organized communal working in their society.

We have so far dealt with the brood in general without
considering the curious fact that from it must emerge the three
different kinds of beings found in every colony—queen,
worker-bees, and drones. Our earlier statements about the
time of development hold for the worker-bee alone. Drones
require three more days to grow from egg to adult bee,
whereas the queen requires five days less than the worker-bee.

Whether a worker-bee or a queen is to develop from a particular egg is decided by the worker-bees nursing it. If they
give the young larva specially nourishing fare in large quantities, and if at the same time they build for it as its dwelling a
cell of a size far exceeding the usual proportions of a bee's
cell, then it will develop into a perfect female. That is, of

course, into a queen, and therefore bee-keepers refer to this particular type of cell as a "queen cell" (pl. VIIIc).

If, on the other hand, a larva is reared in an ordinary narrow cell and fed with meagre amounts of food of a different composition, it grows into a female with underdeveloped ovaries, i.e. into a worker-bee.

But it is the queen who decides, in the process of laying the egg, whether a female (queen or worker) or a male (a drone) is to develop from it. Her ability to do this may be explained as follows:

A queen may reach the age of approximately between four and five years, but only once, in her youth, does she unite with a male on her "nuptial flight". From this time on she carries the sperm of this male well protected in a little sac inside her abdomen. This sac or receptacle (called the spermatheca) communicates through a narrow tube with the oviduct through which her eggs are deposited (see fig. 9). As an egg slides past, the queen, by means of a very precise mechanism, can allow some of the sperms to leave the receptacle and come into contact with an egg, which is thus fertilized. Or alternatively, she may withhold the fertilizing sperm, in which case the egg is laid unfertilized. The fertilized eggs develop into females (i.e. queen or worker-bees), while unfertilized eggs produce only males. Why the sex of

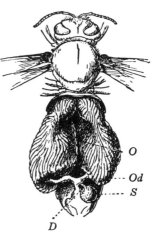

Fig. 9. *Queen bee: abdomen opened from above, with the two ovaries slightly separated.* O, *ovaries*, Od, *oviduct (duct leading out of the ovary)*, S, *spermatheca—receptacle of sperms*, D, *duct into spermatheca.*

the bee is thus dependent on the presence or absence of fertilization, nobody as yet knows. This form of sex-determination is by no means general; on the contrary, it is most exceptional and almost confined to bees. It is the queen who decides whether

drones are to be produced or not, but the worker-bees make
their contribution as well: drones are larger than worker-bees
and consequently larger cells have to be built by the workers
for the raising of the drone brood. Except for their more
imposing dimensions, the drone cells closely resemble ordinary brood and storage cells (pl. viiid). Drone cells have to be
provided before the queen can lay her unfertilized eggs in
them; so here also the workers take the initiative and use the
queen as their tool.

CHAPTER FIVE

The Swarm

SPRING, the time of blossoming and of the most abundant food supply, is also the most prolific breeding time. In consequence of the fast growth of the larvae, the queen's diligent egg-laying leads to a quick increase in the numbers of bees, and thus to a rapid strengthening of the colony. But it does not immediately lead to an increase in the number of colonies as well, because each colony with its queen, as we know, represents a "state" complete in itself, so that the increase in brood increases only the number of its citizens.

However, the number of colonies must also multiply. Not infrequently a whole colony perishes either through disease or through a famine following a bad summer, or through some other misfortune; and if new colonies were not established to balance this loss, bees would soon become extinct.

Every new colony must have a queen of its own, and only after another queen has been provided can a colony multiply itself. This is done by the "swarming" of the bees.

The preparations for this are made on the quiet. During the month of May the workers are chiefly busy building queen cells in which they breed young queens, feeding them on the special diet already described. One new queen would be sufficient, but since the one might meet with an accident, and as it will be easier to destroy a few superfluous queens than to provide a second one at short notice, half a dozen or more queens are bred, the majority of whom are doomed from the start. Sentimentality does not exist in nature.

About a week before the first young queen leaves her cell,

the colony begins to swarm. Again the workers seem to take
the initiative. During the last few days their activities have
begun to slacken, and if theirs is a strong colony, many bees
will rest in front of the entrance of their dwelling, forming
thick clusters. Then, all of a sudden, they become excited, as
if moved by a common impulse. They rush into the hive,
and falling on the honey cells fill their honey sacs. Half the
colony moves out. They hurry out of the entrance hole, their
filled honey sacs serving as provision for their journey into
the unknown. In a mad whirl, flying round each other in
circles, they gradually rise into the air, a huge cloud of bees,
with their old queen flying along with them.

At first their journey does not take them very far. This
time the queen is in the lead; wherever she settles, be it on
the branch of a tree or on some other similar object, there the
whole cloud of bees will collect, settling around her in a thick
cluster (pl. IX), presumably attracted by the royal scent. For
an alert bee-keeper this is the moment to secure the swarm
without much trouble, by collecting and putting it in an
empty hive. If he misses this moment the swarm is usually
lost to him. For while the main swarm hangs from a branch
in quiet idleness, its "scouts" are busily at work, searching in
all directions to find a suitable abode, something like a hollow
tree-trunk, or an empty beehive in another apiary, maybe
miles away. Returning, they now mobilize the swarm, leading it away from the place of its first short rest. Guided by
these scouts towards their new home the cluster of bees
gradually dissolves again, travelling away again in a cloud.
This probably happens at the very moment when the bee-
keeper is just finishing his preparations for hiving the
swarm.

Half the bees have remained in their old hive. They are
now without a ruler. But not many days will pass before the
first of the new queens begins to emerge. She does not, however, immediately replace the departed queen-mother in all
her activities. Emerging from her cell as a virgin, she must
first achieve her marriage flight before she can begin to lay

eggs. A queen is never fertilized inside her hive. Usually within a fortnight after emerging from her brood cell she takes to the air to unite with a drone high up in the skies. After that she becomes a sedate matron, never to leave her home again unless a young queen threatens to dethrone her in the following year: in that case she will rush out through the entrance again, but this time in the midst of a newly formed swarm.

Such is the course of events if a colony sends out only one swarm. In this case the worker-bees destroy the surplus queen cells, killing their inhabitants, after the emergence of the first queen. But it may happen that the new queen also leaves the hive, taking with her another portion of the colony to form a second swarm. Whenever this is to happen, the workers do not kill the remaining young queens immediately after the emergence of the first queen. These young ones do not dare to leave their royal cradles, lest the free queen, who will not tolerate the presence of another queen, should attack them at once. They only push their tongues through little slits in their cells so that the workers can feed them. Now we may hear a strange duet resounding through the hive. The free queen emits a kind of piping sound and the imprisoned queens also make similar noises which, however, from the depth of their dungeons sound like a hollow "quack quack". Bee-keepers maintain that the quacking bees are asking whether there is a queen about, and as long as they get an answering piping, they take good care not to leave the protection of their cells. More recent observations, however, have shown that bees are unable to discriminate between sounds. They are unable to distinguish between piping and quacking and are only receptive to tones in their immediate vicinity through a very finely developed sense of touch. Probably the young queens are prevented from emerging prematurely not so much by the piping of their elder sister as by their perception of her scent. At any rate they are aware of the departure of their rival in the midst of a new swarm, while they themselves remain inside their cells. Only after this has happened do they leave their cradles, one of them staying with the colony as mother of the hive while the rest are killed off.

Occasionally it happens that further swarms will leave the hive and correspondingly more queens succeed, in turn, to the throne. On the other hand, there are years during which a colony may completely fail to swarm, owing either to un favourable weather or to a state of malnutrition.

CHAPTER SIX

The "Battle of the Drones"

LONG before starting to build their first queen cells, the worker-bees have constructed some drone cells, from which the first drones are due to emerge about the beginning of May—"lazy, stupid, fat, and greedy", according to the German poet Wilhelm Busch. Indeed they do not attempt to take any part in the collection of food, an activity for which they are not properly equipped by nature, anyhow. Most of them are too indolent even to help themselves to their own share of the hive's food stores, leaving it to the worker-bees to feed them. The brain of the drone is smaller than that of both worker and queen—we are not left in any doubt as to the intellectual inferiority of the male in this case. The necessity of fertilizing the queen is the sole justification of the drone's existence—each queen requiring but a single drone for this purpose. And yet extravagant nature produces hundreds and hundreds of drones in each colony fated to perish again without having ever gained their object in life; a fate which they share with many a living creature.

As fertilization has to take place in the open, the drones leave the hive to take the air on a fine day, always on the lookout for a queen setting out on her marriage-flight. They often miss the way back to their own hive, entering instead at the first available colony, where they are given a hospitable reception as long as swarming goes on. Towards the height of summer, when the young queens have ceased to fly, and the nectar flow is diminishing, the worker-bees begin to change their attitude towards their bulky hive-mates. Now that males

31

have become useless, the workers start plucking and biting
those very drones whom up to now they have nursed and fed,
pinching them with their firm jaws wherever they can get hold
of them. Grasping their feelers or their legs, they try to pull
them away from the combs, and to drag them towards the
door of the hive. They could not make their meaning clearer.
Once they are turned out of the hive, the drones, unable to
fend for themselves, are doomed to die of starvation. With
great obstinacy they try to force their way back, only to be
received again by the workers' biting jaws, and even by their
poisonous sting, to which they yield without offering any
resistance. For drones do not possess a poisonous sting, nor
for that matter the least fighting spirit. Thus they find their
inglorious end at the portals of the bee dwelling, driven out
and starved, or stung to death, on a fine summer's day. And
this is the meaning of the "Battle of the Drones": not a
sudden upsurge, or a "Massacre of St. Bartholomew", as
some poets, writing of bees, would have it; but a slowly rising
hostility on the part of the worker-bees which may drag on
for weeks, getting fiercer and fiercer all the time, until every
single drone has been killed.

From that time onwards until the following spring, the
females of the colony, left to themselves, keep an undisturbed
peace.

CHAPTER SEVEN

Division of Labour in the Colony

WE have already mentioned in passing that there exists a strict division of labour among the workers of a bee colony: some of them tend the brood while others see to the cleanliness of the hive; others again build the combs, defend the hive, or collect either honey or pollen. One is tempted to draw a comparison between these conditions and those prevailing in human society; we feel compelled to think of a human community with its teachers and policemen, street-sweepers and carpenters, bakers and confectioners. But the analogy remains only superficial. There exists an essential difference between man and bee in regard to the mode of division of labour. With us, when someone has decided on a career he generally keeps to it to the end of his life. Worker-bees, on the other hand, change their activities with increasing age, according to a fixed plan, as long as conditions in the hive remain normal. During their lives they pass through one after another of all the various professions which have been laid down for them in the bee community—each bee starting her career as a cleaner and ending it as a forager.

The whole span of life of a worker-bee, counted from the moment of her emerging from her cell to the moment of her death, may be divided into three distinct periods or stages. During the first stage she busies herself inside the hive tending the brood. During the second stage she has to carry out work of another kind in the hive, including some tasks which necessitate occasional short excursions into the surrounding country. During the third stage, in which she has to collect either pollen or honey, the whole scene of her activity lies out of doors, spread over a wide range, with the hive as its centre.

Each of these main periods contains a number of sub-divisions to which in turn more detailed tasks are allocated. With what degree of accuracy this is done has become known to us in recent years, when scientists have used the only method which was likely to yield reliable information, i.e. painstaking and incessant observation of the individual worker-bee from the day of her emergence from her cell to the very last hour of her life. To carry out such an enterprise called for the use of certain technical devices, as well as of consider-able patience. An ordinary beehive is a dark box and even if glass windows were inserted in all its four walls one could not see the surface of its combs, for these are normally arranged standing in a row one behind the other (pl. IIIa). Therefore one needed, first of all, to build a hive in which all the comb faces could be seen at one glance, so that one could watch what happened inside. Even then it would be extraordinarily diffi-cult to keep one's eye, for any length of time, on one individual bee amidst the bustle of a crowd of many thousands. And it would be hopeless to try to identify a bee whose activities had been watched the day before, or to recognize on her return, a certain worker who had been observed leaving the hive for an outing only a short time previously. The second requirement would therefore be to mark each individual bee in whose doings we are interested, in such an unmistakable way that we should always be able to find her again.

Our first requirement is met by the construction of an observation hive (pl. xa). This is a special kind of shallow hive in which the combs, instead of standing behind each other in the usual way, stand beside and above each other, forming one single large comb as it were, both surfaces of which are visible in their whole extent through two large glass windows inserted in the two broad sides of the hive. The bees are able to pass from one comb to the other by crawling under-neath the wooden frames which serve to separate the two

IX (a) *A swarm of bees collecting round its queen on the branch of a chestnut tree. S, the swarm beginning to settle (photo: Dr. Roesch)*

(b) *The swarm cluster, round the queen*

X (a) *Observation hive with side covers removed. Through the glass window the combs are seen side by side. The bees can move freely from one comb to another under the piles of wood which serve as window frames*

(b) *Observation hive with overhead shelter and passage*

windows. The unusual brightness prevailing in their new
home does not affect their behaviour for long, as they gradually
get used to it. Between one observation period and the next
the windows are covered by wooden boards which, lined with
padding, serve also as protection against the cold at night
The entrance hole to the hive, situated in one of its narrow
sides, leads into the open through a funnel-shaped passage
which protects the observer against any annoyance from the
guards (pl. xb).

For a long time scientists sought in vain for a suitable
method of marking bees. It would be possible to dab a variety
of colours on to them, but the choice offered by our paint-
box would all too soon be exhausted. As an alternative, we
could write numbers on their backs with a fine brush dipped
in white ink, but these would be blotted out in the throng of
the hive and soon become illegible. Taking the good points
of both methods by combining the clearness and durability
of paint spots with the versatility of a numbering system, we
have arrived at a system that appears to satisfy all demands.
All we had to do was to decide that, for example, a white
mark on the front edge of the thorax meant number 1, and a
red mark in the same place, number 2; that blue should
represent 3, yellow 4, and green 5. The same colours when
applied to the hind edge of the thorax mean: white, 6; red,
7; blue, 8; yellow, 9; and green, 0. Now we are able to
write two-digit numbers, as for example the number 12
(white and red side by side on the front edge of the thorax),
or 29 (red left in front, yellow right at the back of thorax).
Should the numbers up to 99 not suffice, then we can dab
the hundreds on the abdomen. In this way, simply using our
original five colours, we can get up to 599. After a little
practice we can read these dabbed numbers as easily and
infallibly as any numbers written in the ordinary way, and
owing to the brightness of the colours it will be possible to
point from a fair distance, even at a bee in flight: here comes
No. 16, or, there goes No. 75! If we have chosen suitable
dyes (dry painters' colours prepared in an alcoholic shellac

solution), the spots will quickly dry and keep for weeks on end without becoming indistinct.

Another little trick was needed to counteract the following effect: any newly emerged bee, who has been numbered in the way described here, and then replaced on the comb, is regularly turned out again by her hive-mates without further ado, probably owing to the unfamiliar smell of paint that adheres to her; oddly enough paint spots dabbed on older bees are completely ignored. Apparently it is only the younger generation which is so carefully picked over for defectives, who might later become a liability in the hive. However these youngest bees have to be marked as well if we want to follow up their complete life history. Fortunately this difficulty is easily overcome by smearing their bodies with a little honey as soon as the paint has dried. This is sufficient to make them welcome to their older hive-mates, which will then lick them over with great devotion, and after this none would dream any longer of harming them. We can now survey their life history.

First period (first to tenth day)

A newly emerged bee looks as ragged as a bird after its bath. The fine, dense growth of hair on its body sticks together in little strands which have to be rearranged. Though still somewhat clumsy in her movements she does this daintily, using her little feet for the purpose. After that her first real activity is to crawl headlong into a brood cell—it need not necessarily be her own—which has just been vacated by some newly emerged bee, to prepare it for the reception of a new egg. She may spend several minutes in it with only the end of her abdomen protruding, then go on to occupy herself in a similar way with several other cells. These cells are cleaned and the inner walls worked over with the jaws; what effect this has is not fully known, but it is nevertheless true that the queen will only lay her eggs in cells prepared in this way. The young workers also sit on the brood cells to maintain their warmth and seem to waste much time in sitting still or walking very slowly up and down the combs. We shall see presently how even this apparently lazy behaviour is of some use to the community.

After a few days, a gland in the head of the bee becomes fully developed, indicating that she is ready for her first job, that of foster-mother. Just as a new-born child cannot digest heavy food and receives everything it needs from the easily absorbed mother's milk, so in the same way bee larvae during their first day are fed with a kind of mother's milk by the foster-mothers. This "milk" consists of a liquid rich in protein which was formed in the head-glands and which is deposited on the floors of the cells. The glands concerned are salivary glands, which change into feeding glands for the good of the community. Their protein content is derived from the reserve of pollen in the hive, which has been consumed by the foster-mothers in order to produce "mother's milk". The older and bigger larvae which can digest somewhat coarser food are fed by the same nursemaids with honey and pollen. This tending of the young entails much work. The rearing of one single larva necessitates between two and three thousand visits to the brood cell by the foster-mother. If one adds up the time taken by one single nursemaid to perform this work, it is found that she has just enough time to rear two or three larvae. Towards the end of this first stage the bee is seen for the first time carefully emerging from the hive. She only goes a very short distance from the entrance, looking round to memorize the situation of her own hive. Soon the flights become longer. These reconnaissance flights soon lead to a knowledge of the neighbourhood, enabling the worker to fulfil duties which from now on lie not only within the hive.

Second period (between the tenth and twentieth day)

The foster-mother period ends with the contraction of the feeding gland. Now, instead, the wax glands reach the height of their development, forming the foundation for the next work, that of building (fig. 10). In addition, workers of this "age group" take over the collected nectar, digest it, and fill

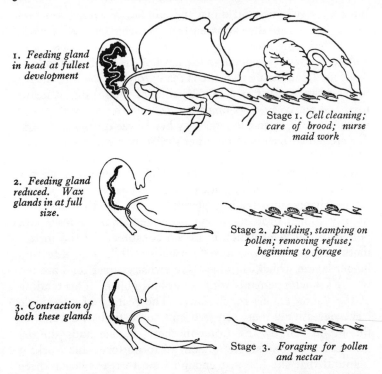

1. *Feeding gland in head at fullest development*

Stage 1. *Cell cleaning; care of brood; nurse maid work*

2. *Feeding gland reduced. Wax glands in at full size.*

Stage 2. *Building, stamping on pollen; removing refuse; beginning to forage*

3. *Contraction of both these glands*

Stage 3. *Foraging for pollen and nectar*

Fig. 10. *Showing stages in the division of labour and corresponding glandular changes.*

the larder cells with it. The cells are padded with the shed "breeches" of the pollen collectors, who work over the walls with head and jaws.

The hive must be kept clean, and this job takes the workers outside. Refuse of all kinds, including the dead bodies of the inmates of the hive, is packed up and carried for a certain distance before being dropped. Many a person who has stood in all innocence at the entrance of a hive has received a few stings.[1] Little does he realize that the attackers are bees of a

[1] The poisonous sting is adapted with a small barb which prevents it from being withdrawn; after being used it tears off, leaving the tail behind. The bee dies of this injury. This is not a cruel arrangement of Nature's as might be

particular and closely defined age group who fulfil their un-written law according to tradition. Towards the end of this second life stage, a required number sit outside the entrance; diligently they examine the incoming bees with their feelers, stop the impertinent wasps and other honey thieves, and hasten to the attack should people, horses, or other monsters approach their settlement.

Third period (from the twentieth day to death)

During this last period, the worker-bee is a forager. She flies forth to collect loads of pollen and nectar from flowers. Should the weather be bad enough to prevent flight, the foragers return unwillingly to housework, but they prefer to wait for fine weather. The proverb "as busy as a bee" arose because as a rule it is only the collecting bees that are seen; those who watch life inside the hive, however, soon appreciate how much time is devoted to idling about.

The bee's span of life

We would be wrong in thinking that a bee about to enter the last period of her life can still look forward to many weeks of browsing among flowers, as a forager. A bee's life is but short; by the time she is allowed to start on her foraging flights a worker is usually past her prime. During spring and summer—the most strenuous periods of foraging—a worker-bee, as a rule, does not live for more than four or five weeks, counted from the moment of her emerging from the brood cell. Threatened by all kinds of dangers during their foraging flights, many workers die before they have reached

---

supposed, but really makes good sense. In the torn-off part lies the nerve centre which controls stinging. The poison gland with which the sting is connected is also situated here. In consequence, the whole stinging apparatus is severed but remains completely alive. If it is not withdrawn at once, it continues to pump more poison into the wound and becomes an increasingly effective weapon against the enemy. For the well populated bee-state, the death of one barren female is no disaster. But the sting is needed far more often against fellow bees or other insects; then it can be extracted again quite easily, as the brittle shell of chitin does not hold it in place as does the elastic skin of vertebrates. Thus a battle with her fellow-insects has no fatal consequences.

even that age. It is not without deeper meaning that the bees are not allowed to start on their foraging until they have performed all their other duties.

A different rule holds for those bees that have emerged from their cells between late summer and autumn. They keep alive through the winter season, during which no new brood is being reared, and may attain an age of several months.

The queen herself lives longer than all the rest. She is able to perform her duties as mother of the colony for a period of four or five years.

An unsuccessful attempt to disturb the colony's rule of life

Throughout the life of a worker-bee there would appear to be a relation between the phase of bodily development which she has reached, and the activity which she is carrying on at the time. To give an example, she begins to act as a foster-mother when her salivary glands are fully developed; as soon as these glands begin to dwindle again, and accordingly her "mother's milk" ceases to flow, she will turn to another occupation; by the time her wax glands have reached their full development she has become a builder. It would be interesting to know whether it is the pre-arranged order in which her organs develop that actually determines the order of the unfolding of her instincts; and whether this order is irrevocable even under conditions that seem to demand its modification in the interest of the colony.

In order to decide this question, we placed a small colony of bees in an observation hive (pl. xa), containing two combs A and B, and with two separate entrance holes, one of which remained closed for the time being (fig. 11, opposite). In the course of eight weeks more than a thousand bees were marked immediately after emerging so that the exact age of each could be told at any time. On a certain day all the bees in comb B were driven over to comb A. After a previously prepared partitioning wall, T, had been inserted between the two combs, the whole hive was rotated through 180° and the second entrance was opened. (See fig. 35, below.) During the sunny hours of the following morning, all the bees which had not yet reached the stage of flying out remained in section A—as was to be expected. The rest, however, which had already performed their first flights, left their comb, returning by their accustomed route, which, under the changed circumstances, led them into section B. In this way a separation into a "young colony" A and an "old colony" B was

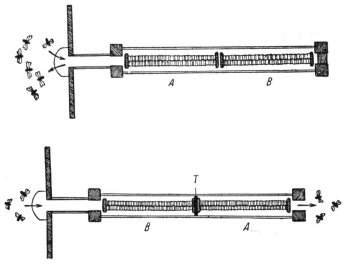

Fig. 11. *Turntable observation hive with inmates divided into old and young bees (horizontal section level with entrance hole).*

Above: before turning; the inside is not divided, only one entrance hole is open.

Below: the hive is turned through 180°, the inside is divided into two parts by the board T; previously all the bees had been moved into A and the second hole is opened. The young bees remain in A, while the old bees fly off to the right; on their return they come in by their usual entrance to the left of B. (after Rösch).

effected within a short time. The "young colony" lacked foragers; there was nobody there to bring in food. Their meagre stores were all too soon used up. At the end of the second day we had to witness the sad spectacle of some bees lying on the ground, starving to death, while other bees started dragging their own larvae out of their cells to suck them dry in their need. Then, suddenly, on the third day, came the turning point. Contrary to all tradition, young bees only one or two weeks old flew out foraging and returned heavily laden with food. Though their fully developed salivary glands stamped them as foster-mothers it was the need of the colony, and not the state of their bodily development, that determined the behaviour of these bees. Their glands had to follow suit, becoming reduced in size in a few days' time. On the opposite side of the hive, in the "old colony" there was a shortage of brood nurses. Here, every bee that was still the least bit youthful stepped into the breach, retaining her fully developed salivary glands long after the end of the customary period.

In another experiment the majority of the builders were removed from their colony by a simple operation. Thereupon this colony was confronted with a situation in which the making of new cells was an urgent necessity. And constructed they were. The building this time was carried out by bees that had long since passed the age of normal builder-bees. Microscopic examination revealed that their wax glands, by now atrophied, had been built up again and had reached an astonishing degree of new development.

The harmony of work

A severe disturbance in the organization such as was caused by this experiment would never occur under normal circumstances. But to a lesser degree, the requirements of the colony constantly change. Sometimes there are more, sometimes fewer, hungry young bees. After a period of bad weather, there may suddenly be a time of rich harvest, and many more bees are needed to gather it in. A rich harvest requires many empty cells in which to store it, and so from one day to the next the need for wax and new combs becomes urgent. The bees meet these varying requirements by developing their glands and feeding juices accordingly. Besides the bees whose turn it is actually to perform a certain kind of work, there are always plenty of others who can join them if required. With some, the head glands develop earlier, with others, the wax-producing organs. The inclination towards a certain kind of work does not depend on a calendar, but is inspired by the need of the moment. It is the job of the idle bees, who seem to wander uselessly up and down the cells, to fulfil this need. They investigate all round, put their heads into one cell after another, and start working wherever they consider it necessary. Thus the smooth running of the bee state is dependent also on the idle members; even laziness can be justified so long as it does not become the principle of life.

CHAPTER EIGHT

Smell and Taste

M AN frequently speaks of his "five senses", although scientists discovered long ago that there are several other senses besides those of sight, hearing, smell, taste, and touch, and that we possess special organs for each of them, just as we have eyes for seeing and noses for smelling. Our sense of balance which keeps us upright even when our eyes are closed is a case in point. Another is the sense of temperature, which has its special perceptor organs situated in our skin, and which conveys to us a sensation of hot or cold, clearly differentiated from what is popularly called "feeling", or sense of touch.

These additional senses play a subordinate part in our lives, and this is the reason why they have only been discovered fairly recently and are not very well known even today.

Again not all of our five familiar senses are of equal importance to us. Loss of sight is a serious injury, and if we spend only a few minutes with a blind man we cannot help noticing how greatly he is handicapped. We may have known someone else for years without ever noticing that he has completely lost his sense of smell—so little is his life affected by the loss. It is after all the sense of sight that dominates in our lives. For a dog or a horse, on the other hand, the loss of their sense of smell would be just as catastrophic as the loss of his eyesight is to a human being.

To the bee, the senses of sight and smell are both of the utmost importance. The first period of her life is spent entirely in the darkness of the beehive, where her eyes are of no use to her. Apart from her tactile impressions it is, in the first place, her sense of smell that guides her in all her activities inside the hive. Later, when as a forager the bee has exchanged this sphere of her activities for the open air, her sight becomes her guiding sense. Out of doors she would be lost without her eyes because she could no longer find her bearings.

The significance of flower scent

If we watch bees foraging in a meadow full of flowers we can notice the following curious facts: we may see one bee hurrying from one clover blossom to another, taking no notice of other flowers, while a second is flying from one forget-me-not to another without paying any attention to clover or any other flower; while a third bee appears to be interested in nothing but thyme. Following the matter up, we find that, over a period of several days, one and the same worker will collect honey from one kind of flower only. Biologists declare her to be "flower constant". This constancy applies to an individual bee, not to the whole colony; while one squad of workers is foraging on clover, other groups flying out, during the same period, and from the same hive, may choose forget-me-nots, thyme, or various other flowers, as the case may be, for their foraging flights.

This flower constancy is good for bees and flowers alike. Keeping to one species of flower helps the bees because they can keep on working in conditions to which they have become accustomed. When a bee alights on a certain flower for the first time, she keeps probing and probing with her outstretched tongue before she finally detects the nectar droplets hidden in its depths; but after the fifth or sixth visit to the same flower she does her business with great promptness; only if one has seen all this can one appreciate the amount of time saved by a bee that has become flower constant. We all know from our own experience that the oftener we repeat a particular process the more skilful we become. Such flower constancy on the part of the bee is more important still for the flower itself, as it forms a necessary condition for prompt and successful pollination: pollen of clover would be useless for thyme, and vice versa.

So far the facts seem clear and simple. Still the existence of flower constancy ought to make us ponder. How is it possible for a bee flying through a meadow in full bloom to pick out, with a high degree of accuracy, all the flowers of one type? Can she be guided by their colour? Only partially. As we shall see later, the bee is able to discriminate between not more than four different colours in the spectrum where we discern a vast range of hues, so her sense of colour cannot be considered a very reliable guide for distinguishing so many different kinds of flowers. Nor can her eyes distinguish the shape of a flower in all its details in the way ours do. But each kind of flower has its own typical scent. Thus we are led to consider the great variety of scents that are present in flowers. In order to assess their importance for the recognition of an individual species we must first find out to what extent the bee has developed her sense of smell.

Training to scent

In order to make the bees answer more of our questions we shall use a method which has proved its use in the study of sense-organs, known as the "training method". Bees are tempted with a small dish of honey placed on a table in the open; soon they start arriving to collect this sweet gift and take it home. As in the case of their visits to flowers, the same insect always returns to its source of supply, and this enables us to train them. Later we entice them with honey into a small cardboard box with a hinged lid and a tiny hole in front (figs. 12, 13). In this box we place a dish of sugar-water. The scented honey is removed, and instead we place a scented flower, a rose for instance, on a little shelf inside the box. Near this box containing food and the rose, we put some empty boxes. In order that the bees, which have an excellent memory for locality, may not get used to one definite position of the feeding-box, we change it round frequently with the empty boxes. Thus all the bees have to guide them is the scent. Will they learn to follow it?

After a few hours a decisive experiment can be carried out. We now set up a number of clean boxes, not yet soiled by bees and so unquestionably alike in scent as in outer appearance. In one of them we put a rose, but no food

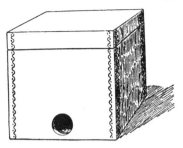

Fig. 12. *Box used for scent training experiments.*

whatever. Within a few seconds it becomes clear that one bee after another is flying towards the entrance hole of the rose-scented box and finally crawling in; whereas not a single bee will enter any of the unscented ones. This behaviour provides

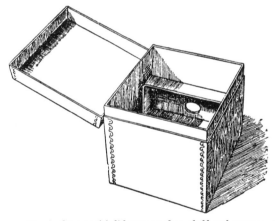

Fig. 13. *Box in fig. 12 with lid open to show shelf and entrance hole.*

convincing proof of the fact that as well as being able to perceive the rose scent they use it as a guide to the place where they have found food.

These results were not unexpected. However, we may use the same method for estimating the relative efficiency of the bee's "nose". In connection with flower constancy and their

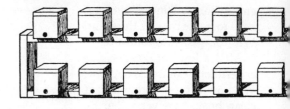

discrimination between different flower types, we wish to find out, first, to what extent bees are able to discriminate between different scents. We therefore set them the task of picking the scent to which they have been trained from amongst a great number of other varied scents.

For this purpose it would not be expedient to use real flowers. Not only does their scent vary in intensity according to circumstances: its very quality (once the flowers have been picked) may change in some way that cannot be foreseen. Nor is a sufficient selection always available.

An excellent method for preserving the fragrance of flowers is practised in the south of France. Pieces of woollen cloth soaked in pure scentless paraffin oil are sprinkled with flowers, e.g. with fresh jasmine blooms, renewed several times. The oil absorbs the fragrance of the flowers, is squeezed out, and put into little bottles which are sent out all over the world to be used in the manufacture of a great variety of perfumery products. In this way the fragrance of jasmine, rose, or orange blossom, among other flowers, may be bought, trapped in little bottles of oil; a few drops of such an oil, sprinkled on to the little shelf of one of our cardboard boxes, are enough to fill its whole inside with a flower scent of extraordinary purity. And apart from these flower essences, there exist a great many others, altogether an infinite variety of scented substances which, in the form of "essential oils", or "volatile oils" are put at our disposal by the perfume manufacturers.

To give an example: we train our bees to one of these essential oils, e.g. the oil of bitter orange peel. For the test following this training over a dozen clean boxes are set up, as

Fig. 14

in fig. 14, this time *all* provided with some scent. One box contains the training scent, whereas all the remaining boxes are filled with a different variety of either natural flower scent or essential oil; none contains any food.

And what about our bees? They approach the entrance holes of every single box, poking their noses into them as it were, but only where the training scent is present do they actually enter the box in order to look inside for their accustomed food. From all the other entrance holes which smell of substances other than their training scent, they will turn and fly off again. They never confuse the training scent with any other unless the resemblance is too close for our own noses to distinguish between them. This may happen with two different kinds of orange-peel oil, one produced in Spain, the other in Sicily. It is hardly possible for an ordinary person to distinguish between the two scents. However, those people who have to cultivate and train their sense of smell as part of their profession have taught us to what extent our senses may be sharpened through practice. An efficient perfume expert testing those two orange-peel oils will tell at a moment's notice which is which. The bees' discrimination is about the same, and they will only occasionally visit the box containing the Spanish oil after being trained to the Sicilian.

The general conclusion to be drawn from the results of these and many other similar experiments is that bees, once they have been trained to a certain scent, not only remember it extremely well but also distinguish it with great accuracy from other scents which are distinctly different from it for a human nose of average ability. Considering that no two flowers smell exactly alike, we are now in a better position to understand the origin of the "flower constancy" of the bee.

Another aspect of the capacity of the bee's organ of smell may be tested in the following way: during a series of successive experiments, bees trained to a certain flower scent are offered their original training scent in ever-decreasing concentration until they are no longer able to select the scented box from amongst the unscented ones. Comparative tests carried out with our own nose enable us to obtain a standard of "olfactory acuity" for the bee, as compared with man. For the small number of scents which have been tested so far, such a comparison reveals that a conformity beyond expectation exists between man and the honey-bee. At approximately the same degree of dilution at which the human nose is no longer able to recognize a certain smell, the bee likewise ceases to detect it. Dogs, deer, and other "sniffing" animals, as well as several insects other than the honey-bee, can boast of much better performance than that.

While both colour and scent appear to combine forces to guide the movements of the foraging bee, the exact part played by each of them in every single case will obviously depend on the intensity of the scent on the one hand and the vividness and shade of the coloration on the other hand. Generally it can be stated that bees are guided by colour from a distance, thus finding the position of the flower, whereas when close they use its scent to make sure that it really is the kind of flower they had been searching for.

This opinion can be corroborated through an experiment in which we train the bees to colour and scent simultaneously, and then test them with the two separately. For example, we feed the bees in a blue box scented with jasmine (fig. 15a, middle box). As soon as the training is complete, we set up, on the left, a box painted blue but unscented, and on the right a box smelling of jasmine, but uncoloured (fig. 15b). We can see how the bees returning from their hive to the feeding place fly towards the blue box, aiming at it with great accuracy from a remarkable distance. On their arrival at the entrance hole, however, they are suddenly startled and, not finding the familiar scent of jasmine, all but a few will pass by the blue box to start on another search, roaming about aimlessly along the row of boxes. The majority of those bees which in their search happen to pass within an inch or two of the entrance hole that gives off the jasmine scent will enter it in spite of the absence of the blue colour. It appears as if the scent as a guiding stimulus had the greater power of persuasion.

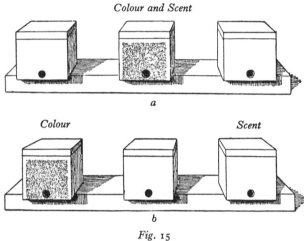

Colour and Scent

a

Colour   *Scent*

b

Fig. 15

This point is borne out by observation in the field. Quite often we can see how a bee, while foraging at a certain flower, approaches blossoms of another kind as well, but only those which for its eyes resemble in colour the coveted flower. Arrived at close quarters, the unfamiliar scent will make her recognize her error at once, and, without coming to rest on the plant, after a moment's hesitation she flies on to a spot where another flower displays its gaudily-coloured sign.

Where to look for the bee's nose

Seldom has science gone so far astray as in its search for the bee's nose. The reason for this is difficult to understand.

The study of the various species of insects showed long ago that a definite relation exists between the development of their sense of smell on the one hand and of their antennae on the other. Moreover we know that they no longer respond to scents after their antennae have been cut off.

Let us describe a case to illustrate our point. We know that in the mating season the males and females of many species of nocturnal moths find each other by means of their sense of smell alone. This is not surprising when we remember that after dark their sense of sight could be but a poor guide towards the other sex. We know that the female moth gives off a scent which attracts the male towards her from quite a long way away. Although a human nose is quite unable to detect such a scent even when very near to the female moth, we can prove that no other sense apart from that of smell can possibly be involved. If a female moth is covered by a glass, in full view of the males that fly over, they do not react at all to her presence. On the other hand, if the female be hidden out of their sight underneath a wire gauze cover, then whole squads of males will arrive and besiege the gauze walls as long as any scent particles are allowed to pass through them. If we lift the cover and remove the female herself, then the males will continue to besiege the place where she has been sitting while her perfume still adheres to it. In certain species the scent glands of the female moth are attached to each side of the abdomen and form two tiny "scent bottles" that produce a scent which, though not perceptible to our own nose, is attractive to the male. It is not difficult to amputate these scent glands without greatly impairing either the appearance or the mobility of the female. The way the male moth loses all interest in the female from the very moment in which this operation is completed, affords us a deep insight into the psychological make-up of these insects as compared with our own. The female moth, though fluttering about in a most lively manner and looking quite unchanged to our eyes, simply ceases to exist for the male, who will start, instead, to try and copulate with her amputated scent glands, now motionless masses lying on the floor, which, for him, appear to represent the essence of the living female being.

In the case of these moths the well-known relation between feelers and sense of smell is developed to such an extent as to produce a striking difference in the external appearance of the two sexes: the female, who remains passive throughout the whole affair carries a pair of very delicate and slender feelers, whereas those of the male, dependent as he is upon his sense of smell during his search for his mate, are enormously enlarged (fig. 16).

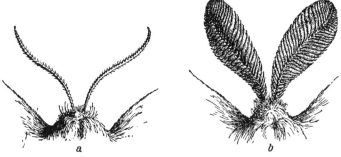

Fig. 16. Head and antennae of moth. (a) *female,* (b) *male*

Deprived of these antennae, the male is no longer able to find the female, even if she is quite close to him.

In spite of this and other similar evidence, some naturalists have gone on searching for a nose on wings, legs, abdomen, and other unlikely places. It cannot be disputed that insects whose feelers have been amputated cease to respond to scents; nevertheless some people have attributed this lack of response to the severe damage which the insects are supposed to have suffered through the amputation of appendages which are so full of nerve fibres. They suggest that, without necessarily losing their sense of smell, such insects would be bound after such a severe shock to show listlessness and general lack of response.

However, this interpretation misses the mark. This may be proved by two simple experiments carried out with honey-bees (pl. XI).

Let us feed a bee from a dish of sugar-water placed on a piece of grey paper. Around the feeding-dish, a few drops of some scented liquid, such as peppermint oil, have been sprinkled. Close by we have placed three more pieces of grey paper, each provided with an empty glass dish and some scent other than peppermint oil, e.g. oil of thyme. The bee, finding her food close to the scent of peppermint all the time, is consequently being trained to seek for this particular scent. After some time we perform a test the object of which is to find out whether the training has been completed; we remove the food, putting down four new grey squares, *all* of which are now provided with *empty* glass dishes; on one of these squares a few drops of the original "training scent" (peppermint oil) have been sprinkled—and on the rest an equal number of drops of the "contrasting scent" (oil of thyme). The bee, taking her bearings from the scent, alights on the paper sprinkled with peppermint oil in search of food. We next repeat the test with the same bee after removing its feelers. The apparent unconcern of our bee after the operation might lead us to believe that insects generally do not feel pain. Continuing her search for the food-dish, the operated bee will go on flying from one square to another, hovering over each of them in turn. She is unable to select the square with the peppermint scent from the squares sprinkled with other scents, and will alight now on this square, now on that, entirely at random, without making a final choice.

In spite of this inability we do not get the impression that this bee has suffered a severe shock. Indeed we can prove by another experiment that the amputation of her feelers has not made her listless or indifferent. We feed another bee on a blue square, with some empty dishes on yellow standing close by—that is, we train her to come to blue. If we now make a test with this bee after her feelers have been cut off, she will still rush towards the blue square, alighting on it and searching for food in its now empty dish. This proves that the operation of removing her feelers has by no means affected her general ability to react. All she has lost is the ability to take

XI (a) Through feeding with sugar water, a bee is trained to the scent of an essential oil. After the amputation of her feelers she can no longer distinguish the plate covered with training scent from the other scented plates. The photograph shows her flying low over a scented plate. She flies from one to another fruitlessly searching for the training scent

(b) Control experiment: a bee trained to blue flies decidedly towards this colour even after both her feelers have been amputated. She searches for the customary food in the empty glass dish, paying no attention to the other three glass dishes standing on yellow paper nearby. Her reactions have not been affected by the operation

XII (a) A bee's feeler, enlarged about 20 times. It is composed of twelve independently movable sections

(b) One section of a bee's feeler very much enlarged. The light spots are thinner parts of the chitin armour (organs of smell), together with centres of smell and countless hairs, the organs of touch

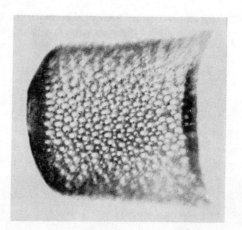

her bearings from a scent. In other words, her organ of smell must be located in her feelers.

But this organ is constructed very differently from that of man. In man it is situated in the depth of the nasal cavity, where a great number of nerve fibres end in the delicate mucous membrane of the nose. It is here that the odorous substances that are breathed in take effect. Just as our visual impressions are conveyed from the eye through the optic nerve to the brain, so our olfactory impressions are conveyed from the nose through the olfactory nerve to the brain, where we become conscious of them.

Insects have no such nose. Their breathing openings, located in parts of their bodies other than the head, are not suitable for the purpose of smelling. Obviously the olfactory organ, being an important and sometimes even a guiding sense organ, is most suitably situated in front of the head. In insects this is where the outstretched antennae (compare pl. vb), into which extend the olfactory nerves coming from the brain, are placed. Odorous substances carried by the air, that can easily reach the endings of the olfactory nerve fibres in the surface of the mucous membrane lining the human nose, cannot so easily reach the nerve endings in an insect's feeler. The surface of the latter, like that of the rest of its body, is covered by an armour, as we have seen in previous chapters. To allow the odorous substances to gain access to the olfactory nerve endings, this armour enclosing the feeler is perforated by a great number of extremely narrow tubes (the "pore ducts"), whose openings when seen under a high-powered microscope appear as innumerable luminous spots covering the entire surface of the feeler. While pl. xIIa shows the feeler of a bee magnified twenty times, pl. xIIb shows a single joint of this feeler even more highly magnified. If we use a microtechnique specially adapted for the purpose we can make a longitudinal cut through such a joint and thus expose the endings of the most delicate branches of the olfactory nerve just where they enter the tiny pore ducts. We now recognize that those narrow tubes which seemed to open out

to the surface are in fact closed against the outer world by
very delicate membranes, the so-called "pore plates", that
form part of the general armour of the feelers. These membranes, though thin enough to allow the odorous substances
of the air to pass through them, nevertheless serve to protect
the very delicate nerve endings from being dried up.

Owing to the presence of an entire forest of minute tactile
hairs, which we may see dispersed between the olfactory pores,
the feelers, known to be the bee's most important organs of
smell, serve also as her most important organs of touch. Such
a double function, if we only come to think of it, must have
peculiar consequences. It certainly makes no difference to the
human nose whether the object it smells is short or long, round
or square. The odorous substances bring no information
about the shape of the object by which they are emitted, when
they reach the back of the nasal cavity. It is quite different
with the bee, however. A bee, whose feelers, in the darkness
of the hive, touch an object in order to examine it—be it a cell
of the combs smelling of wax, a newly laid egg, or one of her
grubs—is bound to perceive the two different impressions of
touch and of smell in very close association. Bees may therefore be expected to perceive a *smell "plastically"*. While we
ourselves are aware only of one sort of impression of a "smell
of wax" for example, whether this be emitted from a hexagonal
cell or from a little waxen ball, there may exist for the bee a
"smell of wax associated with a hexagonal shape" quite different from the "smell of wax associated with a spherical
shape". We may say that we ourselves, being accustomed to
associate our visual with our tactile impressions from early
childhood, are able to see "plastically" in exactly the same
way as the bee can smell "plastically". It is possible that the
efficiency of the bee's organ of smell has reached a very high
degree of perfection because of this peculiar ability of hers.
However, her mode of sensation will always remain incom-
prehensible to us, being outside the scope of our experience.
For the bee, who has to rely to such a great extent on the
senses both of touch and of smell during her work inside the

dark hive, the ability to smell "plastically" may represent a definite addition to the rest of her sensory capacities.

Taste and smell

In the county of Salzburg, people sniffing at a bunch of flowers can as often as not be overheard exclaiming "What a pleasant taste!" without there being the slightest doubt that this careless mode of utterance is really meant to express their delight in a pleasant smell. On the other hand, a great many people express themselves almost as incorrectly—without realizing the fact—when they praise the "taste" of a joint they are eating, or the "flavour" of a glass of wine they are drinking. We are in fact quite unable to draw a sharp line between the two sensations of taste and smell. An explanation of this fact is found in the close proximity of the two corresponding sense organs, as well as in the way in which each is stimulated.

Both senses have this in common that they will respond only to an immediate contact with the object to be smelled or tasted, and that the quality of the sensation depends upon the chemical composition of the object. In the case of our sense of taste this is quite obvious. If we place a lump of sugar or a grain of salt in the mouth, it is soon dissolved in saliva, and in this dissolved form stimulates the organs of taste which are distributed over the surface of the tongue. In a comparable way we can only smell evaporating substances, that is to say, substances whose surfaces continuously give off minute particles which are distributed in the air. Such particles are invisible to us because of their minute size. However, we can check their evaporation in other ways, e.g. by placing a scented object on a pair of very sensitive scales; we should then notice a steady if almost imperceptible decrease in weight. Some strongly-scented substances, such as camphor, exist which give off particles from their surface so rapidly that after some time nothing is left of quite a large piece. Such evaporating particles, along with the stream of inhaled air, are carried into the nose, where their contact with the olfactory nerve endings produces olfactory sensations, which differ in quality according to the chemical composition of each substance.

In fig. 17 we see the position of the organs of smell and taste as they appear in a longitudinal section through a human head. Whatever we eat or drink must pass from the mouth

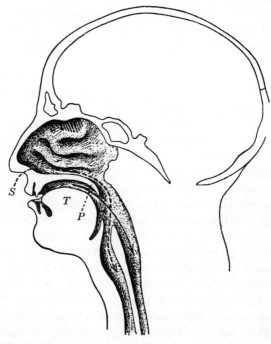

Fig. 17. *Section through a human head. The solid arrow shows the food passage, the dotted arrow the breathing tubes.* T, *tongue, centre of the sense of taste. The darker shaded patch,* S, *in the nasal cavity is the centre of the sense of smell.* P, *roof of the palate.*

cavity along the pharynx into the oesophagus (path shown by black arrow). This path is crossed by the stream of inhaled air passing through the nose over the soft palate and through the larynx into the windpipe (see dotted arrow). The tongue is the seat of our sense of taste, while our sense of smell is located in the small part at the top of our nasal cavity shaded

in black in fig. 17. Odorous substances must pass this point
as they are sucked in with the inhaled air. On the other hand,
all those varied odours which emanate from the food and
drink we take into our mouth, are bound to reach this point
from behind, after passing over the soft palate, though we are
not conscious of this fact. It is not until our olfactory sense
has been eliminated—perhaps through an illness—that we
begin to realize how little remains of the so-called "pleasant
taste" of our food and drink, when this is assessed by the
tongue alone. Our sense of taste conveys to us not more than
four qualities—those of sweet, sour, bitter, and salt. These
four, however, may combine with one another to create any
number of new taste sensations. All other "aromas", however, are conveyed to us by our sense of smell.

In the bee, the organs of taste are located inside the mouth
cavity and the sucking tongue (or "proboscis"). However,
we do not know if taste and smell are as closely associated for
them as for us, as we cannot put ourselves in the place of a
bee. For the rest, the functioning of the two sense organs in
man and bee shows a degree of conformity which is truly
remarkable considering the great differences in structure. In
both cases, the organ of smell is adapted to perceive those
minute particles that evaporate from scented substances, and
responds to them with a degree of sensitivity that puts to
shame all our modern chemical test methods. No chemist,
with the finest of reagents, would be able to detect such
minute traces of certain substances as are sufficient to evoke a
marked olfactory sensation in man and bee alike. It is this
high degree of sensitivity that defines the sense of smell as a
distance-conquering sense, the minute evaporating particles
representing volatile messengers, able to bridge the gap between stimulus and sense organ. Compared with the sense of
smell, the sense of taste appears dull; its task consists solely
of testing the chemical quality of the food that has been
taken in.

An old Latin proverb states that there is no point in dis-
agreeing about taste: *de gustibus non est disputandum*. If two

owners of gardens cannot agree as to which has grown the biggest cucumbers they are likely to come to a decision in the end, if only by calling in a third party. But it would be quite meaningless if two people had a dispute as to whether the addition of sugar did, or did not, improve the taste of coffee. The results of a few experiments have been sufficient to convince us that the same substance need not taste the same to different people. It is only natural for a human being to believe that a taste which is most pleasant to *him* is indeed superior to all other tastes; and he will probably stick to his opinion, no matter what decision has been made by anybody else.

If we cannot agree among ourselves as to the pleasantness or unpleasantness of a certain taste, how can we expect to agree with the insects? Indeed, we should consider it most remarkable were we to find agreement among the two groups about certain aspects of taste.

Throughout the animal kingdom we find a high regard for sweetness. However there are great individual variations in the keenness of the sense of taste. While the minnow, a small freshwater fish, is able to recognize the sweetness of a sugary solution at a concentration of only one-hundredth of what would be just recognizable as sweet for man, we know of certain butterflies the taste organs in whose feet are as much as a thousand times more sensitive to sweetness than the human tongue Since the nectar produced by flowers is nothing but a sugary juice, recognized and consumed by the bees because of its very sweetness, the possession of a sweet tooth, so to speak, would appear to be a most important factor in the life of a bee. However, we are quite wrong if we expect the bees to be exceptionally sensitive to sweetness; exactly the opposite is true. They are unable to distinguish between pure water and a solution of about three per cent cane sugar that tastes distinctly sweet to us. A bee would refuse such a solution even if she were on the point of starvation, though she would rush towards any droplet of sugar-water that was concentrated enough for her to recognize it as such.

To illustrate the differences between the various species I show, in fig. 18, a drawing of a bottle containing one litre of pure water side by side with the amount of sugar that has to be dissolved in it to produce the degree of sweetness just perceptible to each of the following: the feet of a species of butterfly highly sensitive to taste (*a*), a minnow (*b*), a man's tongue (*c*), and a bee's proboscis (*d*). Whereas a butterfly is

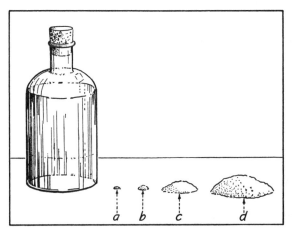

Fig. 18. *The bottle contains one litre of water. Beside it are different sized heaps of sugar which must be dissolved in the water for the following to appreciate a sweet taste:* (a) *butterfly*, (b) *fish*, (c) *man, and* (d) *bee.*

able to utilize any amount of sugar, however minute, for its nutrition, there is good reason why the bee's sense organs should be comparatively insensitive to this taste. It is as a winter store for the hive that the bees collect the nectar. A weak solution of nectar would not keep and would therefore be quite useless as provision. A bee would no more deposit a weak solution of honey within the cells of her hive than a housewife wanting to prevent the formation of mould would economize on sugar in jam-making. Nature has created the honey-bee with taste organs insensitive to sweetness so as to spare her the temptation of acting in a way that would defeat her own biological purpose.

The plants for their part meet the bee's desire for durable food halfway by producing in their flowers a surprisingly high sugar content, usually of between forty and seventy per cent. Bees cannot be deceived by saccharin or by similar substances which, though tasting quite like sugar to us, yet lack its nutritional value. This does not mean that they are more intelligent than we are. The simple reason why they do not take so kindly to these substances which seem so sweet to us is that they cannot taste them at all.

Quinine is sometimes smeared on the fingers of a child that insists on sucking his thumbs. It tastes so bitter that its application beats all other educational devices for curing this bad habit. Yet bees will drink with the greatest relish a solution of sugar diluted with an amount of quinine that would make it completely unpalatable for us. There are other bitter substances as well to which bees are much less sensitive than we are.

It would be easy to enumerate still further differences between the sense of taste in bee and in man. However, as we are not concerned here with writing a cookery book for honey-bees, these examples may suffice.

CHAPTER NINE

The Bee's Eye and how it works

Colour vision

SUPPOSE the reader is breakfasting out of doors during a visit to the country. There is some honey on the table, and bees occasionally appear there, attracted by the scent. This situation offers an opportunity for carrying out a simple experiment for which nothing is required except a piece of red paper, two pieces of blue paper of the same size, and some patience.

Let us remove the honey-pot and place a few drops of honey upon one of the blue papers which we place on the table. It will not be long before some bees find the honey, and suck it up. After filling their honey-stomachs they will fly back to their hive, returning to our table a few minutes later, to get more from this plentiful source of food. We allow them to fly to and fro a few times. Then, removing the honeyed paper, we place, on either side of its original position, two new papers: namely, the red, and the other piece of blue paper, but without dropping honey on either of them this time. The bees, while showing no interest whatsoever in the red paper, will swarm round the blue paper and even settle on it in spite of the fact that they do not find any food on it, and that there is no honey scent to attract them to it (pl. XIIIa). They have remembered that food had been offered on *blue*, and moreover, are able to distinguish between the red and the blue colour.

It has been concluded from such experiments that bees possess some kind of colour vision. This conclusion is, however, premature. The matter is by no means as simple as all that.

One occasionally finds people whose colour vision is more or less deficient as compared with that of a normal human being. There are also those rare people who are unable to perceive any colours at all. To the eye of such a "totally colour-blind" person, even a brilliantly-coloured landscape would appear as its photograph in monochrome appears to us. He would be able to perceive the objects in the great variety of their shapes, but only in grey tones; differences of colour would appear to him as differences of brightness only. Now, if we present our red and blue papers to a totally colour-blind person, he will be able to distinguish quite well between the two, and will not confuse them. He will not, however, distinguish them by their colour—which will always remain a closed book to him—but by their relative brightness; since red will appear to him as a very dark grey, almost as black, while blue will appear to him as a light grey. His impression of the situation is therefore quite different from our own, comparable to the one which we receive through the colourless photograph in pl. XIIIa. Thus for his eyes each colour possesses a definite degree of brightness, if no other quality.

This shows that our previous experiments do not allow us to decide for certain whether the bees have distinguished the red paper from the blue by its different colour, or by its different degree of brightness—as any totally colour-blind being would have done. Therefore, if we want to come to any definite conclusion, we shall have to arrange our experiment in a slightly different way.

Our question is: does the blue paper appear as a colour to the eye of the bee, or as a shade of grey of a certain degree of brightness, as it would to a colour-blind human eye? As we cannot foresee in which particular shade of brightness our blue paper would appear to a totally colour-blind bee's eye, we have to find out whether the bee can distinguish it from *every* possible shade of brightness. In order to do this, we have to use a whole series of grey papers, leading, in fine gradation,

from pure white to absolute black. If we place a clean blue
sheet without food in the midst of such a series of grey papers,
arranged in an arbitrary order, in front of bees previously fed
on blue, they will still fly towards the blue sheet as if quite
sure of their goal, and settle on it (pl. xiiib). This shows that
they can, indeed, distinguish the blue as a colour even from
the entire gamut of grey shades.

In performing such an experiment it is advisable to display
the grey papers from the very start during the feeding on blue,
since otherwise, at the decisive moment, the bees would be
taken by surprise by the unwonted sight, and would therefore
react with less certainty. For the same reason, a little glass
dish is placed on every one of the papers from the beginning,
while only the dish on the blue paper is filled with food. In
order to eliminate any possible influence of a honey scent we
decide to use sugar-water in preference to honey as food.
Since bees possess a strong memory for places, it is also a good
plan frequently to change the position of the blue feeding-
paper among the whole series of papers. In this way, bees
arriving at the table in search of the food-dish will soon learn
to make use of the colour as their only reliable guide. Within
a very short time, they can be "trained" to blue well enough
to fly directly towards the dish on blue, whatever its position
on the table, even if it is clean and empty. Nor do they allow
themselves to be distracted by the glass plates with which we
cover all our papers in order to make sure that it is the *sight*
of the blue paper, and the sight alone, that determines the
choice of the bee. Some people had indeed suggested that the
bees might have been guided by a *scent*, which, imperceptible
by human noses, might be emitted by the blue paper. It is
obvious that such a scent, if it existed, could not be perceived
through a sheet of glass.

Our experiment is equally successful if we train the bees to
yellow instead of to blue. However, if we try to use a pure
red paper we are in for a surprise. Bees which have been
fed on red, will, in the test experiment, select black and
dark-grey squares just as often as red ones from amongst the

squares of our chequer-board arrangement, and the most elaborate training, however long continued, will not make them change their behaviour. Red is, in fact, confused with black by the honey-bee; it is not perceived as a colour but as a very dark grey, exactly as it is perceived by the eye of a colour-blind man.

There are other aspects of its vision in which the bee's eye is not only equal but superior to that of a normal human being. It is only through the ingenuity of our physicists that we know about the presence of certain rays in the sunlight which cause no visual sensation in our eyes—the so-called "ultra-violet rays". Bees can see these rays, and what is more, it has been proved by experiments that they perceive this "ultra-violet" as a separate colour, different from all other colours. Thus, the red-blindness of the bee is compensated for by its ultra-violet vision.

One thing is now clear: bees see colours in a way which is different from our own. This fact becomes particularly obvious if after having trained some bees to a certain colour we set them to the task of distinguishing the training colour from a number of others. We do this by displaying, in the test experiment, our training colour side by side with other coloured papers of strongly contrasting hues, instead of presenting it among various shades of grey, as we had hitherto done. It is here that the bees make mistakes which could not happen to a human being gifted with normal eyes. After being trained to yellow, they will settle on orange-coloured and on yellowish-green papers as well as on all the yellow shades, thus revealing to us that all these colours, so unlike each other to our own eyes, must appear similar to them. Likewise, all shades of blue are confused with violet, mauve, and purple. On the other hand, bluish-green as well as ultra-violet are perceived as separate colours by the bees, who can also distinguish each of the two from both yellow and blue. Fig. 19 gives a good illustration of the different impression made by the world of colours on the eye of the bee on the one hand (below), and on our own eye on the other hand (above).

If we let a beam of white sunlight pass through a prism and then fall on a screen, its various rays are sorted out according to their wavelengths and the band of the spectrum appears in all its coloured magic, as known to everybody in the rainbow. *Red, orange, yellow, green, blue,* and *violet* are only names for the most striking colour shades which, however, blend into one another, passing in gradual transition through many intermediate grades. Where we perceive such a great variety, the bee discriminates but four colours: *"yellow," "blue-green,"*

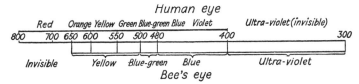

Fig. 19. *The colours of the spectrum. Above: as they appear to the human eye; below: to the bee's eye. The numbers indicate the wave lengths of the beams of light (in thousandths of a thousandth millimetre) at given points of the spectrum.*

"blue," and *"ultra-violet"*. Obviously we can have no conception of what the nature of her sensation is at the sight of any of these colours. We do not even know the inner experience of those nearest to us when they call a colour by the same name as we do. For no man's eye has ever looked into another's mind.

The eye of the bee and the colour of flowers

Anyone who believes that the flowers of the field in their beauty were created with the sole purpose of giving delight to man's eye should study the relation between the occurrence of certain colours among flowers, and the colour vision of their winged visitors, and he will become quite humble.

To begin with we are struck by the fact that by no means all of the so-called "flowering plants" produce real "flowers". Many plants, like grass or corn, the conifers, elms, poplars, and a few others, produce small, inconspicuous and scentless blossoms which do not secrete any nectar, and are not often visited by insects. The transfer of their pollen, effected by the wind, is more or less left to chance; it is only assured to a certain extent by the fact that a dry, easily dispersed pollen is produced in extraordinary quantities. In contradistinction to these "*wind-pollinated*" plants there exists a group of "*insect-pollinated*" ones which, with the help of their nectar secretion, attract foraging visitors that transfer pollen from one blossom to the next; a speedy and more dependable method of pollination. The blossoms of plants belonging to this group are either remarkable for their scent or conspicuous for their gay colours, or sometimes for a combination of the two. These are the "flowers". Naturally, we feel tempted to assume a close connection between the two phenomena. Just as an inn-keeper puts out a gaily-painted sign to attract the attention of the traveller, and induce him to call at the inn for his own refreshment and the landlord's profit, so it might be the purpose of all those gay little flags displayed by the flowers to guide the bees from afar towards the place where nectar flows, and where they are invited to call to the advantage of both host and guest. If it were true that the floral colours were thus intended to impress the eyes of the pollinators, then we should expect a relation to exist between the nature of these colours and certain peculiarities in the colour vision of their visitors. Such a relation is most strikingly in evidence.

Long before there was any detailed knowledge of the colour vision of bees, botanists had noticed, and with due surprise commented on, the rarity of pure red flowers. However, a "true" or scarlet red happens to be the only hue which does not impress the eye of the bee as a colour, and would therefore not render any flower conspicuous for this particular pollinator. Most of the so-called "red" flowers of this part of the world, such as heather, rhododendron, red clover, cyclamen, etc. do not, in fact, show that "true red" hue of which we are talking here; practically all of them display a purple or mauve colour which to the bee's eye must appear as some shade of blue.

Perhaps plants find it difficult to produce a scarlet colour in their petals? This cannot be the correct explanation, since such scarlet coloration is exceedingly common among tropical flowers, some of which we like to keep as ornamental plants in our hothouses and gardens just because of their peculiar colouring. On the other hand we have no grounds for

Fig. 20.   Humming-bird at a flower of a climbing plant (Manettia bicolor), *hovering and sucking honey.*

assuming that the vision of tropical bees differs from that of our own native bees. However, in the tropics these brilliant red flowers are not pollinated by bees, or by any other insect for that matter, but by small birds such as humming-birds, which hover in front of them (fig. 20) sucking up, through their long beaks, the abundantly-secreted nectar which provides their nourishment; a fact long known to students of ecology. Moreover, it has been proved that the very shade of "true red" to which the bee's eye does not respond is perceived as a particularly brilliant colour by the eye of the bird.

There exists another, third, relation between the colours
of flowers and the responses of their guests, which had been
known for many years, and had been much discussed by
scientists before being explained through recent experiments.
Those flowers, few in number, which approximate to a "pure
red" coloration in our native flora, like red campion and some
of the Dianthus family, are, to a great extent, pollinated,
not by bees, flies, or beetles, but by butterflies, whose long
tongues enable them to suck up nectar from the bottom of
corolla tubes which, in these species, are particularly deep.
Such great depth seems to indicate a special adaptation on the
part of these plants for pollination by these long-tongued
insects. And in the light of our present knowledge, butterflies are the only insects which (in contrast to bees) are able to
perceive red as a colour.

We could hardly have asked for more. It looks, indeed, as
if the various colours of our flowers reflected the red-blindness
or otherwise, of their respective visitors. It was to be expected
that the ultra-violet perception of the bee should likewise be
reflected in the development of the colours of flowers. That
this is so has since been confirmed by experiments, though
these relations are, of course, not obvious for our own ultra-
violet-blind eyes. It was the poppy blossom that gave us our
first surprise in this respect. In spite of the fact that it is one
of the few flowers of our countryside that is coloured a "true
red", the poppy is eagerly visited by bees. We ourselves are,
of course, unable to see that its petals reflect the ultra-violet
rays as well as those red ones which are of no significance for
the bees. Thus, the poppy looks red to us, while it appears
as an "ultra-violet" flower to the honey-bee. This fact should
remove, once and for all, the basis of any possible discussion
about the poppy having seemingly acquired a colour which
cannot be perceived by its visitors. Even the majority of
"white" flowers appear coloured to the bee. The reason for
this is odd; in order to appreciate it we must undertake a short

digression into the field of physical optics. We know that sunlight is made up of various light rays of different wave-lengths, which, if separated by means of a prism, for example, can be made visible as separate colours to our eyes; by mixing these colours again with the help of a second prism we can make the light appear white once more. If, however, by means of a suitable filter, we cut out one of those colours before reuniting all the different rays, then the mixture of the remaining rays will no longer appear white to us, but as a colour which is "complementary" to the colour of the removed part of the light beam. A similar law holds for the vision of the bees. Another great surprise was provided by the discovery that nearly all our white flowers act as filters, cutting the short-wave, ultra-violet rays out of the sunlight—an effect which our own eyes cannot perceive—so that to the bee these flowers appear in a colour which is "complemen-mentary" to ultra-violet: that is to say, as *bluish-green*. This is of some importance, because bees do not remember a "white" surface reflecting all the colours visible to their eyes, including of course the ultra-violet rays, quite so well as a coloured surface, for which reason it is more difficult to train them to feed on "white". And in fact this sort of "white" is hard to find in the world of flowers.

Where we see the white starlets of daisies standing out against the green of our lawns, there we must imagine blue-green starlets set up against a background of pale yellow, shining into the eyes of the bee. White apple blossoms, white campanula, white convolvulus, and white roses—all these display a gaily-coloured inn sign for their colour-loving guests.

But the nature lover's delight in all these flowers will hardly be diminished by the thought that their colours are intended for eyes other than his own.

The structure of the eye

If we compare two people with each other we may find that though colour vision may be perfectly normal and alike in both of them, yet their eyes may differ greatly in visual acuity.

One of them may be able to pick out details of a far-distant object with a keenness of eyesight that would do credit to a Red Indian, while the other, being extremely short-sighted, will, without his spectacles, display a helplessness which is a provocation to every caricaturist. Even the most careful ana-tomical dissection will not teach us anything about the ability of an eye to perceive colours, because this ability depends upon details of the eye's inner structure which are of such fineness as to defy even microscopical analysis. On the other hand, the ability of an eye to perceive the shape of an object as distinct instead of blurred depends so directly on its coarse anatomical structure that anatomists are able to judge from its outer appearance alone whether an eye belongs to a short-sighted or to a long-sighted person.

However, if we dissect the eye of a honey-bee, or of any other insect for that matter, in the hope of learning something about its efficiency through analysing its anatomical structure, we shall find that all the experience we may have gained in the course of studying the human eye will be of no avail, because the structure of the latter is basically so different from that of an insect's eye. To find out how nature, through using entirely different ways and means, has contrived to reach the same goal, in two beings as fundamentally different from one another as man and the honey-bee, makes a particularly interesting study for the naturalist.

The structural details of an insect's eye are of such fineness and great variety as to put to shame those of the human eye. To understand them completely would require a thorough and scrupulous study based on difficult physical and other scientific arguments. Fundamentally, the difference between the two types of eyes may be explained as follows:

The human eye may be compared to a photographic camera. The aperture in the iris of the human eye, called the pupil, corresponds to the opening in the front wall of the camera. In strong sunlight the iris muscles contract so as to reduce the diameter of the pupil, thus protecting the inner eye against the entrance of too much light, just as the aperture of the diaphragm in our camera can be reduced in order to exclude excessive illumination of the plate or film. The lens of the camera corresponds to the lens of the human eye in both shape and function. If we look at a distant luminous point (A in fig. 21) that emits light in all directions, our lens collects all those rays that enter through the opening of our pupil, bringing them to a focus in one single point (a), on our retina at the back of our eye. If we imagine a second luminous point, B, appearing above the first one, then all light rays coming from it would

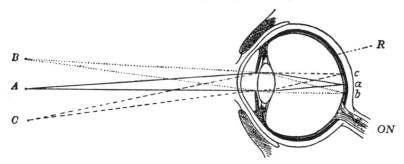

Fig. 21.   *Human eye*. R, *retina;* ON, *optic nerve*.

again be collected by the lens, being brought to a focus on a point of the retina (b), situated slightly below the first point; likewise, all the light rays coming from a third point C, situated below A, would be concentrated in a third point (c), also inside the eye, but above the other two. It is left to the reader to imagine these three points as three stars sparkling in the sky, or, if he so prefers, as three candle-flames shining one above the other, along a vertical line. This consideration holds good for any luminous point, whether self-luminous or only illuminated by sunlight or by artificial light, because in this latter case the point would reflect, in all directions, the light falling on it, with almost the same effect as if it emitted the light rays itself.

Now we may think of every object appearing in our field of vision as being made up of a great number of separate points to each of which we may apply the rules of focussing which we had deduced for our first three luminous points, A, B, and C. In this way, our lens throws an image of the object at which we happen to look onto the retina at the back of our eye. This image, though inverted and diminished, shows all the details in correct proportion, just as the image thrown by the lens of our camera on to the film is inverted and reduced in size, but, nevertheless, lifelike.

It is in the utilization of this image that the essential difference between eye and camera is to be found.

In the camera, the image produced at one definite moment is caught on the plate, to be preserved for ever. In our eye the place of the photographic plate is taken by the retina; it is through the agency of the retina that we become conscious of the distribution of light and shade throughout the image, now dissolving, now reappearing again, according to our ever-changing field of vision. The most important part of this, our retina, consists of a very fine mosaic of rod-shaped elements, each so slender that several hundreds placed side by side would just cover the span of one millimetre. Each of them is connected with the interior of our brain by a single nerve fibre; the entire mass of these extremely fine fibres combines to form the optic nerve which extends from the eye to the brain. Each luminous point focussed onto a retinal rod causes a message to be taken along its corresponding nerve fibre, through which it is conveyed to the brain, and it is here rather than in the retina itself that the conscious sensation is born. This holds good for a single flash of light in the dark as well as for the infinite number of individual points that fuse into the single image which completely fills our field of vision in daylight. Because the image on our retina is upside down, some people have wondered why the world does not appear to us to stand on its head. However, this question is meaningless, if only for the reason that it is not in the retina at all that the image becomes conscious to us. This happens in the brain, at a time when, in accordance with the course taken by each individual nerve fibre, the respective position of the separate parts of the image has long been changed.

To those of our readers who are not satisfied with this exposition, it may be comforting to hear that a human being who has fully understood the innermost working of the mysterious process of vision has yet to be found.

The eye of the bee—like the eyes of all other insects—is not provided with pupil, iris, or lens. The retina at the back of its eye is comparable to the human retina except that the image thrown on to it is produced in a different way. A strongly convex eye rises from each side of the bee's head (pl. vb facing p. 16). Seen through a magnifying lens of high power, the surfaces of these eyes appear to be divided up into a great number of exquisitely neat little facets (pl. xivc), thus indicating in its outer appearance the difference of its inner structure from that of the human eye. This difference becomes much clearer if we carefully cut an eye in half (fig. 22, pl. xiva). The faceted surface of the eye is made of the same chitin which forms the exoskeleton of the insect's body. As an outward protection it corresponds with the cornea of our own eyes. Directly attached to each facet of this cornea is a crystal-clear, cone-shaped body, the crystalline cone. This cone collects all the rays of light which come into its field of vision and passes them on to the retinal rods, which together form the retina. Each facet with its attached cone and relevant retinal rod is called an optic cone or *ommatidium*. Now a bee's eye is made up of many thousands of such *ommatidia*, which are packed together tightly and which, even more important, have their axes slightly inclined towards each other, so that no two of them point in exactly the same direction. Each of these little cones, like an arm in a dark sleeve, is surrounded by a black mantle which is impervious to light.

Within the visual field of such an eye, let us again imagine one single luminous point, sending out light-rays in all directions, some of which are bound to strike the eye's surface. Only in the one *ommatidium* that points directly towards the light source will the light-rays, progressing in a straight line, have a chance to pass through the whole length of the tube so as to reach the retinal rod. All the rest of the *ommatidia*, being set at a slightly oblique angle, absorb the light-rays in their black mantles before they can reach the light-sensitive retina. A second luminous point, situated above the first one, is bound to lie in the line of the axis of an *ommatidium* situated above the first one; a third luminous point below

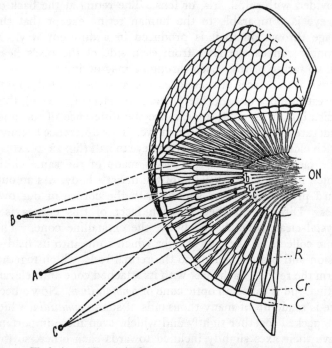

Fig. 22. The bee's eye (diagram). C, *cornea.* Cr, *crystalline cone.* R, *retinal rod.* ON, *optic nerve. The points* A, B *and* C *in the field of vision correspond with the points* a, b *and* c *on the retina, where the inverted image becomes upright.*

the other two will be intercepted, and directed towards the retina, by a third optic cone situated below the other two (fig. 22). The same consideration holds good for all those numerous points which may be imagined to combine in forming the surface of an object. Each *ommatidium*, as it were, selects that tiny part of the whole visual field which is circumscribed by its own projection.

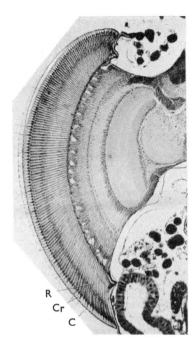

(b) Photomicrograph of the impression on the retina of a firefly's eye (magnified *120* times). A church can be seen through a window. A capital R cut out of black paper has been stuck on to one of the window-panes

XIII (a) Section through a bee's eye. C, cornea; Cr, crystalline cone; R, retina. (In the upper part a small part of the cornea has become detached in the preserving fluid)

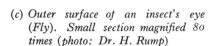

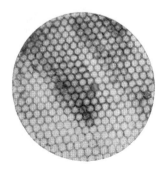

(c) Outer surface of an insect's eye (Fly). Small section magnified *80* times (photo: Dr. H. Rump)

XIV (a) Bees, which have previously been fed on a blue paper ★, search for food on a clean blue paper (left), while they ignore the red paper (right)

(b) Proof of ability to distinguish colour. A blue paper lies in the midst of pieces of grey paper of various shades. On each sheet is an empty glass dish. Bees trained to blue collect on the blue paper, proving that they can distinguish this colour from the various shades of grey

That this is another method of producing a retinal image is clearly shown in fig. 22. However, in this case it is not an inverted image, as in the lens eye; since the pattern of their little images on the retina tallies exactly with the spatial pattern of the corresponding parts of the real object, an upright image is formed by this eye.

This particular difference between the two types of eyes has been much discussed. It is not, however, of intrinsic importance, as it only represents the natural consequence of the two different ways in which the retinal image is formed. In the bee, the contents of the entire visual field, after having struck the surface of the eye, are immediately being cut up into a mosaic pattern of tiny parts of the image; each of these parts is then separately conducted, through its optical cone, towards its retinal rod, and further on to the brain. In our own eye, the lens projects an inverted image which remains coherent until it is being split up, in the retinal rods themselves, into a mosaic pattern which is then conveyed to the brain. In both cases it is the task of the brain to reunite the parts of the mosaic in such a way as to produce an integrated whole within the mind.

The drawing in fig. 22 has been simplified as well as magnified in order to demonstrate the formation of such an image. Plate XIIIa, on the other hand, gives a more realistic view of an insect's eye, showing how numerous the optical cones really are, and how elegantly and neatly arranged. It shows a section through the eye of a bee as photographed through the lens of a microscope.

Visual acuity and perception of form

The next thing we should, naturally, like to know is: with what degree of acuity does an insect's eye, structurally so different from our own eye, perceive an object in its surroundings? There are various ways of finding a clue to this.

The best way of elucidating a point is by direct observation. It has been possible, not only to observe an image directly, as it is formed on the retina of a glow-worm by its *ommatidia,*

but even to take a photomicrograph of such an image, showing a window and the view from it (pl. xivb). We clearly
recognize the crossbar of the window, the letter R (cut out of
paper) sticking to the window pane, and a church tower in the
distance—all this as actually seen through the eye of the
glow-worm. This particular little insect has been selected for
our experiment because its *ommatidia* are fixed at their front
ends and so do not become disarranged if the whole eye is
cut off with a fine scalpel. It is thus possible to separate the

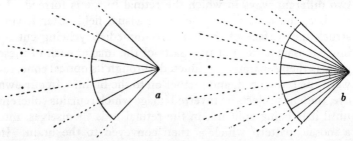

*Fig. 23. Sharpness of vision of the insect's eye depends on the number of
wedge-shaped sections.*

ommatidia in their entirety from their retina so that the image
formed by them can be viewed and even photographed through
the lens of a microscope. This image strikes us as rather hazy if
we compare it with our own normal perception of the object.

An anatomical examination of the eye yields similar results.
A simple consideration shows that the greater the number of
ommatidia available for the reproduction of a given visual field,
the more accurate in all its details the retinal image will be;
just as in a mosaic picture, where the greater the number of
stones used, the more accurate will be the representation of
the object. The eye shown in fig. 23, under (a), is unable to
perceive the three black points in front of it as separate units
because they fall into the field of vision of a single *ommatidium*
supplied with a single retinal rod. The eye in (b), on the
other hand, is able to perceive them as three different impressions because in this case each of the points is depicted in a
different *ommatidium*. It is obvious that the resolving power

of an insect eye increases in inverse proportion to the visual angle subtended by each of its *ommatidia*. In the eye of the bee, this angle is approximately 1°. Accordingly, a bee is unable to perceive two points as separate stimuli if they are less than 1° apart. A human being with keen eyesight, on the other hand, is able to distinguish two points as two individual stimuli if they are separated by as small an angle as one-sixtieth of a degree. It is therefore obvious that the visual acuity of the bee compared with that of man must be con-

sidered as being very poor indeed. The naturalist must realize that many of the beautiful forms in nature remain hidden to his favourites. Perhaps he would like to discover to what extent this is so. As the bees cannot tell us, we must again adopt the

Fig. 24. *Shapes that can be distinguished easily and certainly by bees.*

training method to find out. By this means we can easily train them so that they can distinguish between the two shapes shown in fig. 24 with great certainty.

Even after prolonged training, bees seem to be quite unable to distinguish between such figures as triangles, circles, squares, and rectangles (fig. 25, upper row) which to us appear so obviously different from one another. It is even more surprising that they should confuse all the figures in the lower row of fig. 25. On the other hand, they can easily learn to

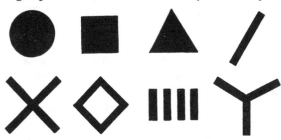

Fig. 25. *Bees cannot distinguish between the shapes in the top row, nor between those in the bottom row. But they can distinguish those in the top from those in the bottom.*

distinguish each of the figures in the lower from every single one in the upper row. From these and other similar experiments, carried out with various modifications, we may conclude that the decisive factor of discrimination, from the bee's point of view, is the extent to which the figure is "divided up"—which also goes hand-in-hand with its relative amount of outlines and contrasts—a factor which is of little consequence for our own discrimination of such forms. All figures distinctively broken up into small black-and-white areas, and, accordingly, possessing a very broken outline, look very much alike to the bees, just as, on the other hand, all plain solid shapes with unbroken outlines resemble each other in their eyes. It is for this reason that bees that have been trained to distinguish between certain shapes have sometimes proved unequal to a task which according to our own ideas should have been very easy to fulfil. They see shapes in a different way because their sight organs are immovable. A bee cannot roll her eyes, nor can she focus on an object that arouses her interest. Her eight to ten thousand little eyes are fixed in the head and point in different directions. When in flight, she can take in the whole panorama below and around her. The impressions which each single eye receives in passing change very rapidly.

If we release flashes of light in a dark room in quick succession, we get the impression of flickering. If we attempt to follow more than twenty such flashes per second, our eyes are incapable of distinguishing them separately. They become merged into an impression of constant light. This method is, of course, used in films; single pictures on the strip follow each other so rapidly in each second that our eyes see uninterrupted movement. We do not notice that in actual fact there is darkness between each fraction of a second, during which time the movement is carried on from one picture to the next. If there were a cinema in the bee state, the apparatus could not work in the same way. The bees would have to see two hundred single pictures in every second if they were not to complain of flickering. Bees' eyes can take in ten times as many single impressions as our eyes during the same period. This is very useful when it comes to seeing a succession of objects or rapid movements which take place under their eyes when in flight. What they cannot see in space is made up for by their appreciation of movement in time. Therefore it is understandable that they pay less attention to immobile shapes and forms than to movement within their field of vision, though they are specially adapted to appreciate rich patterns of light and colour.

This is how their vision may be explained. To attain certain knowledge, or to view the world even for one moment in the way a bee sees it, must remain unfulfilled wishes for the inquisitive naturalist.

The perception of polarized light

Most people know nothing about polarized light. They are not very interested in it, as they need scientific apparatus to help convince them how often we see such light without realizing it. At school we learnt that light comes in waves or vibrations, that it moves at tremendous speed, that the waves travel transversely across the beam of light and that, in the natural light of the sun, the wave front can be of any size and changes constantly and quickly in an irregular manner. In fig. 26a a beam of ordinary light is shown coming

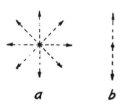

a   *b*

Fig. 26. *Simplified diagram to show direction of waves in* (a) *ordinary,* (b) *polarized light.*

towards us. The lines indicate some of the changing directions of the vibrations. In the case of polarized light, all the vibrations lie in one definite plane (fig. 26b).

Polarized light is not uncommon in nature. The sun's light caught in a mirror, or on water, or reflected from a wet street is partly, and under certain circumstances completely, polarized. The blue sky is full of polarized light, though we do not notice it as our eyes cannot distinguish between ordinary and polarized light. To insects, however, and other arthropods, polarized light is something special. They can even distinguish the direction of its vibrations, which they use to help them in their orientation. This applies equally to bees; their capacity for doing this was only discovered a few years ago.

Polarized light can also be produced artificially, for instance with a Nicol prism. Recently, large transparent filters have been invented which completely polarize the rays which pass through them. With gadgets like these it is easy to determine whether light (of the composition of which we know nothing) is polarized, and also the direction of its vibrations. Fig. 27 will make this clear. A long strip of polarizing material is cut and placed directly across a beam of light, in such a way that the light passes straight through. We cannot appreciate immediately that light treated in this way is really polarized. Neither is it apparent if we put a second filter in the same position on top of the first (a), because in this case, since the light is polarized by the first, it can pass through the second unhindered. The part which is covered up appears only a little less transparent because the strips are only slightly coloured, but two of them obviously absorb more light than one. If one strip is rotated across the other, however, the light will become absorbed, as in (b) and (c), until finally it disappears altogether by the time the strips are at right angles (d). When

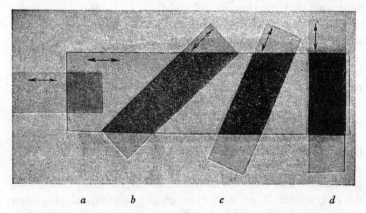

a   *b*   *c*   *d*

Fig. 27. *Showing what happens when the two strips of polarized material are moved from a parallel position to one where the planes are at right angles.*

they are at right angles, the second strip is opaque to the vibrations coming through the first. In an oblique position, only part of the light penetrates the second strip; the more the strips diverge, the less will be the intensity of light.

To appreciate what takes place in insects' eyes, we dispose the strips somewhat differently: isosceles triangles are cut out of polarizing material in such a way that only light whose

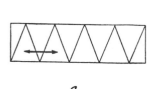
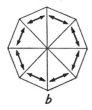

a   *b*

Fig. 28.   (a) *Strip of polarizing material, showing the pattern cut out for the formation of a star-shaped filter;* (b) *star-shaped filter.*
The double arrows indicate the direction of polarized light.

vibrations are parallel to the base lines of the triangles is transmitted. These triangles are then arranged in the shape of a star (fig. 28). If one looks through this at a light source which emits ordinary light, all the triangles will appear equally bright (fig. 29a); we do not see that the light coming through it is polarized and is vibrating in different planes. If one looks at a source of polarized light (fig. 29b) the triangles form a

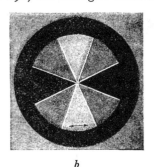

a   *b*

Fig. 29.   *View through the star-shaped filter,* (a) *of a light source emitting a natural light,* (b) *of a light source emitting polarized light; its direction is indicated by the double arrow.*

pattern of different intensities which varies according to the direction of the vibrations of the incident light.

A similar process goes on in the faceted insect eye which can thus distinguish the different directions of polarized light. On p. 75 we discussed how the incident light is directed

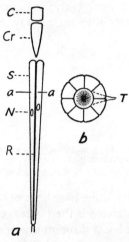

Fig. 30. (a) *A single ommatidium from the compound eye of the bee (cf. fig. 22), very much enlarged.* (b) *Section through the single eye at the line a—a, still more enlarged.* S, *sense cell.* N, *nucleus of the sense cell.* R, *retinal rod (the innermost part is probably the most sensitive to light).* Cr, *crystalline cone.* C, *cornea (chitin covering).*

through each individual eye to the retinal rods. By careful observation and with a strong magnification it can be seen that each of the retinal rods is made up of a group of eight cells and in consequence is octagonal in shape, like our star-shaped model (fig. 30). The similarity is not merely superficial, for the effect on the waves of light is the same. This apparatus makes the faceted eye superior to our own, as it enables its owner to distinguish polarized light.

CHAPTER TEN

Orientation: how the Bee finds her way about

SUPPOSE we are standing in front of a large apiary, with twenty colonies housed side by side in an equal number of hives, all looking very much alike. While thousands of worker-bees are rushing off on their foraging flights, darting about like arrows, others can be seen returning, each making unhesitatingly to her own colony, to disappear again through the entrance hole. Suppose we catch one of these home-bound bees and after marking her with a spot of paint shut her up in a little box and carry her away, setting her free a mile away from the hive. An observer left with the hives will report to us that our marked bee has entered her old hive again only a few minutes after her release.

We feel tempted to postulate the existence of some kind of magic force, strong enough to guide the bees safely home even over a great distance. When we look more closely into the matter, however, their achievement appears less miraculous.

A bee that has not yet reached the stage when she begins to leave the hive—for example a young worker-bee still serving as a brood nurse—carried out and released in the open, however close to the hive, would be unable to find her way back home. She can only do this after first getting to know her surroundings. This she normally does when about ten days old (see p. 37), at which time she starts on her first outings, which are easily recognized as orientation flights. There can be no question here of either a rapid departure or a "bee-line" return; cautiously she hovers up and down, hither and thither in front of the apiary, facing her own hive all the time, very much as we do when we take a good look at our hotel in some strange town so that we may find our way back to it later. Her next excursions take her a little further afield; bees caught at this stage and released outdoors will find their way home from anywhere in the close neighbourhood of the hive but not from a greater distance. Soon flights are gradually extended further and further until they cover the colony's entire foraging territory two or three miles in every direction. Carried off to still more distant places, even an old forager bee will not be able to find her way home. Therefore the faculty of orientation is not due to any inborn gift but rather to an ability to learn gradually to memorize the position of the hive. It seems most likely that, in doing so, the bees, like ourselves, use the more striking visual landmarks, such as groups of trees, houses, and the like, as a help in taking their bearings.

We know of one more circumstance that fits in well enough with our own experience to make us doubt the existence of a mysterious force that could direct the bees on their flight home. It is the fact that they frequently go astray. How many bees, having as yet incompletely memorized their bearings and therefore unable to find their way back home, are left to perish in the open fields? We shall never know. One thing we do know—that in large apiaries with rows and rows of hives all looking very much alike, bees will frequently enter the wrong hive. There is a very simple way of proving this. All we need to do is to open a hive and mark a few hundreds of its inmates with spots of white paint. After a few days many of these bees will be seen frequenting neighbouring hives or even flying in and out of colonies housed at a fair distance from their own. Bee-keepers who are aware of this state of affairs disapprove of it, because such stray bees are not always allowed into a hive without being challenged by the guards, who can recognize by their smell that they are strangers. They may then be bitten and stung and often fatally wounded, or at best, valuable time will be lost which, in the interest of the bee-keeper, ought to have been spent on nectar collecting instead.

But something far worse might happen if the queen herself ever mistook a strange hive for her own on her return from her nuptial flight. Her error would not only mean certain death for herself but, unless a new queen could at once be substituted, it might spell disaster and ruin for the entire colony.

For this reason it has long been a custom with some bee-keepers on the continent to paint the front walls of a row of hives in different colours, thus making it easier for the bees of each colony to recognize their own home. This method however has not yet been commonly applied because there has as yet been no general agreement as to its efficiency. To-day we have no doubt that this painting of the front walls is an excellent device for keeping bees from straying into other hives. We also know the reason why its efficiency had been doubted for so long. Had not the colours meant to guide the eye of the bee been selected by and for human eyes? Obviously, a bee-keeper who paints his rows of hives alternately yellow, green, and orange, or one who juxtaposes blue, mauve, and violet, or even red and black, cannot expect to have any success, as the colours in each of these groups are too much alike in the eyes of the honey-bee (see p. 67).

Importance of colour and scent as guides for homing bees

Though a well-chosen colour certainly helps the bee to recognize her own home, no amount of guesswork can tell us exactly how much colour helps her in her orientation. This can only be discovered by experiments.

As the most suitable starting point for such an experiment, we select a large apiary stocked with a number of hives all of which look exactly alike. In a certain place in this apiary we set up several empty beehives side by side. We then mask the front wall of one hive with a large piece of blue sheet-metal, while covering its alighting board with a smaller piece of the same material (see fig. 31a, middle hive). The hive on the right is similarly provided with a yellow covering, while the one on the left-hand side retains the original white paint used on all the hives of this apiary. After introducing a colony of bees into the blue hive we shall have to wait for several days. The eye of the bee is quite capable of distinguishing blue, yellow, and white from one another. If outgoing bees do in fact make use of the blue colour for recognizing their home, then it should be quite easy to guide

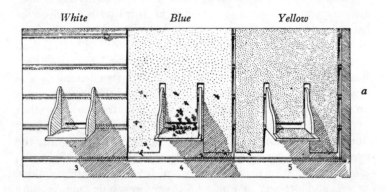

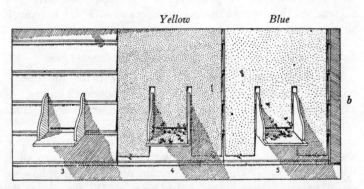

Fig. 31. Proof that the bees use the colour of their hive as a means of orientation. (a) The middle hive is inhabited, the neighbouring hives are empty. The middle hive is covered with a blue metal sheet, the right hand one with a yellow sheet. In order to be able to change colours without changing the actual metal sheets (and thereby transferring the particular bee scent that clings to them), the blue sheet is painted yellow on the reverse side, while the yellow sheet is blue on the back. (b) The metal sheets are reversed, thus changing the colours. Some of the homecoming bees fly to the empty, but now blue, hive.

them into the wrong hive by interchanging the blue and yellow covers. However, we must not forget to take one necessary precaution. In the course of their coming and going, numerous bees will have settled on the blue sheets during the last few days, particularly on the small one that covers the alighting board of the occupied hive. Consequently these sheets will be impregnated with their scent to a degree perceptible even by the human nose. If we interchanged the blue covers of the occupied hive (fig. 31a, middle) with the yellow covers of the empty hive (the one on the right) and the bees chose the blue hive (now unoccupied), then they might have been guided by the scent adhering to the blue sheets, as well as by the blue colour. Having anticipated this source of error we have painted the back of each of our blue sheets yellow, and the back of each of our yellow sheets blue. In this way we can avoid any exchange of sheets in our test. All we have to do, while leaving the sheets in their original places, is to reverse them. Thus the occupied hive is turned yellow, and the empty hive blue without any bee scent being transferred to it (fig. 31b). As soon as this has been done we see the returning bees approaching the empty hive which is now blue, some of them even passing through its entrance hole, while others, stopping short of the entrance as if they missed the familiar smell of their colony, soon find their way to their old home, in spite of its changed appearance, having apparently been led by their sense of smell.

Yet this experiment is not wholly satisfying. All it can tell us is that some bees after all do take notice of the colour of their hive while others again behave as if they did not trust it completely.

Why should we assume, at any rate, that the bee when taking her bearings should note the colour of *her own hive only*? Suppose she noticed the colours of the two neighbouring hives as well, memorizing the fact that her own blue hive is flanked by a white one on the left and a yellow one on the right? If this were so, we would be bound to create confusion if we changed the order of colours in our experiment—

a white hive on the right with a yellow on the left. If the bees who had noticed this change now reverted to their sense of smell for their orientation, then we should have to modify our experiment accordingly. We propose to do this in the following way:

Having restored the original position (as in pl. xva), we now repeat our test experiment so as to reverse the sheets—turning them from blue to yellow—on the occupied hive only, while removing the sheets from the right-hand hive altogether. These are then fixed in the reverse position to the left-hand hive, making it appear blue. In this way the original order of the colours to which the bees had become accustomed, remains unchanged: a blue hive in the middle being again flanked by a white one on its left and a yellow one on its right-hand side. The effect of this new arrangement is striking: all the homing bees which had gathered in front of the apiary during the short interval that was needed for the transfer of the sheets will now without a moment's hesitation begin to invade the wrong hive, misled by its blue colour. This will go on for several minutes (see pl. xvb) during which time all out-flying bees leave the yellow hive and all returning bees enter the blue one.

The outcome of our test has proved to us that colouring the hive with a suitable paint may have a decisive influence on the orientation of the bee at the apiary. The results of our experiments have been confirmed on a larger scale in practice. If the hives in our apiary are painted in colour shades that bees can easily distinguish they rarely go astray. If we mark with paint spots a few scores of bees which occupy such a hive, we can see them leaving, as well as entering, none but their own hive for a period of days or even weeks on end. Likewise their queen will experience no difficulty in finding her way during her nuptial flight as well as during the orientation flights that precede it. From 1920 onwards, the fathers of the monastery of St. Ottilia in Upper Bavaria have carefully recorded the behaviour of all queens hatched in their large model apiary. During the years 1920 and 1921, before any

XV The bees are attracted to the wrong hive if blue remains in the same relative position to the other colours

White   Blue   Yellow

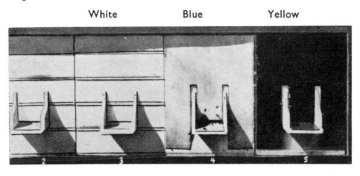

(a) The normal order of colours to which the bees are accustomed

(b) The metal sheet on the usual hive (no. 4) has been turned round so that it appears yellow, the sheet on the hive to the right (no. 5) has been removed and turned round (blue instead of yellow) and is placed on hive no. 3 to the left of the usual hive. All homecoming bees make for the uninhabited, but now blue, hive no. 3

White   Blue   Yellow   White

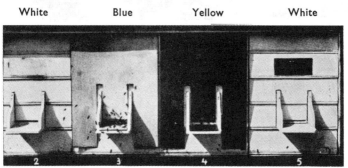

XVI Bees with their tails up surrounding the entrance hole, drawing attention to it with the scent emanating from their upturned scent organs. The homecoming bees recognize the scent of their hive in the current of air that they produce by fanning with their wings

of their hives had been painted, sixteen out of a total of twenty-one young queens got lost. Afterwards, all hives were covered with suitable paint of various colours, taking into account the bee's ability for colour discrimination. During the first five years of this practice, not more than three out of a total of forty-two young queens were recorded as lost.

The bee-keeper who wants to make practical use of this theoretical knowledge should bear in mind that blue and yellow, black and white are the contrasting colours most easily distinguished by bees.[1] He should restrict his painting to these colours, and he should ensure that if two hives standing in the same row are painted the same colour they should be separated by at least two hives painted a different colour. Wherever a colour is used more than once, care should be taken that it does not recur as part of the same colour pattern, because we know that the bee uses the colouring of the neighbouring hives as a landmark, as well as that of her own. It is a bad practice to paint only the entrance board; the whole front wall of the beehive should be coloured. In the light of our present knowledge, a bee-keeper who sticks to these rules (see fig. 32) makes homing as easy for his bees as he possibly can.

Colour is not the bee's only navigational aid. In the case of an unpainted hive, the bees take their bearings from the

---

[1] Bee-keepers willing to make use of the latest scientific discoveries may increase the number of available colours by using both *lead white* and *zinc white*. The differences between these two paints which to our own eyes appear to be identical is that they reflect different parts of the spectrum: while lead white reflects a great amount of ultra-violet light which is invisible to us, zinc white absorbs it. Lead white which reflects to approximately the same degree all the various rays visible to the bee, is bound to appear "white" to her, while zinc white, like most of our white flowers, must appear "minus-ultra-violet" or blue-green to the bee (see p. 71). It has been established in experiments that bees can, in fact, distinguish these two whites from each other quite as well as they can distinguish blue from yellow. Apart from these two, white paints are not recommended because they either absorb or reflect only part of the ultra-violet rays, for which reason it is difficult to say in what colour they will appear to a bee. Hives painted with such white paints cannot produce a clear-cut colour effect and have probably been responsible for many failures in the past. It is possible that a paint exists that would appear "ultra-violet" to the bee's eye, though up till now, it has not been discovered.

nearest corner of the apiary or from some other landmark, memorizing the distance between it and their hive. Above all they are led by the scent of their own colony. It is not yet known to what extent the various components of this scent, as for example the odour of the combs or the scent of the brood, are responsible for this. No doubt the odour produced

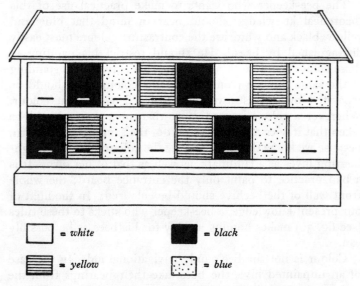

	= white		= black
	= yellow		= blue

Fig. 32. An arrangement of colours that will simplify homing.

by the worker-bees' own scent organs is of great importance. In a later chapter we shall deal with the part played by this scent in communicating the location of a rich source of food (compare p. 115). Even when they are quite near their hive, bees make use of their scent organ. We may watch them sitting, either on the alighting board or in the entrance, with their abdomens facing outwards. In this position they will be seen to open their scent pockets and waft their scent towards the arriving bees with fanning movements of their wings. They do this with particular vigour whenever it is most important to mark their hive, as for example on their first outings in early spring when, after the long rest of winter, the memory of the hive's position has faded from their mind, or when, after swarming, the colony has moved to another home the location of which has as yet to be memorized (see pl. xvi).

The sky compass

The Vikings had no compass. For their long journeys across the oceans they relied on sun, moon, and stars. The stars can be used in two different ways for purposes of orientation, depending on whether one goes on a long or a short journey. Let us imagine that we are in an unknown part of the country, strangers in a lonely house and wanting to find another house a quarter of an hour's walk away but invisible owing to hilly country. Someone shows us the direction. In order not to lose it, all we have to do is to keep in the same position with regard to the sun during our journey. We are then bound to move in a straight line. This is a method often used by animals, first observed in the case of certain ants. If one of these insects leaves her nest on reconnaissance she always moves at a certain angle to the position of the sun and consequently goes in a straight line. On her return journey she does the reverse. A convincing test can prove that the sun is really her only guide across country. If an ant is shaded with an umbrella and at the same time shown the sun through a mirror from the opposite side, she immediately changes direction and sets off on a different course.

This method is of no use over long periods as sun, moon, and stars change their positions. If the Vikings had not known this, they would have gone round in circles on the high seas.

It is an astonishing fact that bees also use the sun as a reliable compass to fix their position, and do, at the same time, take the time of day into consideration. It is true that they have no watch, but they have a sense of time which will be described in chapter 12. That bees really make use of the position of the sun in this way can be seen by the following experiment: a feeding place is set up at a place 200 yards to the west of where we are standing and there from two to three dozen numbered bees are fed with sugar-water from morning till evening. A little scent (such as lavender oil) is added. After a few days, the hive is closed early one morning and transported many miles away to completely different surroundings. Four identical feeding-tables with sugar-water and lavender oil are then placed to the west, east, north, and south, 200 yards away from the hive. An observer sits near each table and watches each bee as she approaches the dish. In the changed surroundings there are no visible signs to enable the bees to discover the points of the compass (see pl. xvii). Also the hive itself is no landmark as it is turned round into a different position, with the entrance hole changed from the east side to the south. Soon, in spite of this, several of the numbered bees, and gradually most of them, make towards the observation point in the *west* whilst only a very few make the mistake of flying towards the feeding places at the other three points of the compass. They must have been guided by the sun's position when searching for the new feeding-place in unknown country, as they always took the same direction. Moreover, they must have taken the passage of time into account, for during their last foraging flights the previous evening, the sun had been in the west, but during the experiment the sun was in the east.

For this experiment to work it is unnecessary to train the bees to a certain feeding place for days on end. One sunny summer day the observation hive was placed somewhere in the country and the entrance hole was not opened before midday. Forty-two bees were numbered at a feeding place 180 yards away to the north-west between three and four in the afternoon and fed there until eight in the evening (fig. 33a). When the bees awoke next morning ready for a new flight, they found themselves twenty-three kilometres away from their former feeding-place, at the edge of a dredged lake, in quite different surroundings, three feeding-places having been set up in addition to the one in the west. In spite of this, bees

(a) *View from the westerly feeding table, F, looking towards the east. The hive is behind the trees and houses, the big lime tree in the middle of the picture lies half way along the flight*

(b) *View from the westerly feeding table, F, looking towards the hive after it had been moved. It stands in the middle of an open field behind the two figures which show up light against the dark wood in the background*

XVIII (a) *The star-shaped filter is mounted in a metal frame so that it can be moved towards any point of the compass and adjusted to any height. Elevation and compass bearing can be read off on two semicircular scales*

(b) *Views of the sky through the star-shaped filter in eight different directions at 45° above the horizon. Photographed on September 25, 1949, at 10 a.m.*

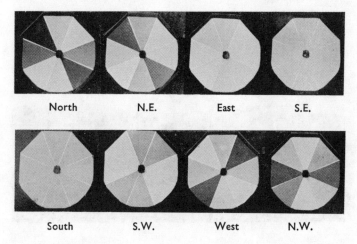

which had been numbered and fed the *afternoon* before now arrived in the *morning* in the following numbers: fifteen to the feeding-place in the west, two to the north, two to the south, and not a single one to the east (fig. 33b). Most of them arrived between seven and eight in the morning. Therefore in flying to their feeding-place in the west they experienced first the sun in front of them in the evening and then behind

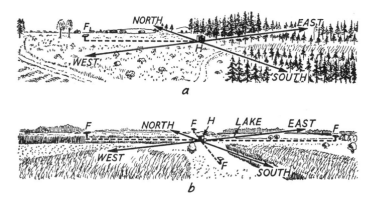

Fig. 33. (a) *The observation hive* before *the change of position.* F, *feeding-place* 200 *yards away from the hive to the north-west.* (b) *Hive after change of position, with four feeding-places.*

them in the morning. If they observe the sun on their evening flights, then they know which angle to keep with the sun in the morning and during each succeeding hour in order to go the same way, thanks to millions of years of experience of the whole bee race.

The moon and twinkling stars which guided the Vikings in the night sky mean nothing to bees, as they stay at home at night. But under the blue sky by day, they are superior to any human navigators, as their eyes recognize polarized light and its vibrations. We have already obtained an idea of how patterns are produced through polarized light in the cells of individual eyes (pp. 83, 84). They are strongly contrasted if the polarization is complete, less contrasted if the polarization is only partial, and the pattern of light alters with change of vibrations. Polarized light comes from the blue sky, and its intensity and vibrations depend on the position of the sun, according to its height in the heavens. This can be proved easily by setting up a star-shaped filter (figs. 28, 29, p. 83) which can be rotated and tilted (pl. xviiia) and adjusted towards different points of the compass. Each direction will show its special pattern (pl. xviiib). We must realize that flying bees keep their position not only by using the tiny portion of the eye that faces directly towards the sun, but by means of their thousands of little eyes which take in patterns distinct for each point of the compass and dependent on the position of the sun. Thus with their composite eyes they embrace the whole expanse of the heavens; they are so to speak optically tied to it and each smallest deviation from their course is registered a thousandfold.[1] If a hill or some other object comes between them and the sun, it is enough for them to see just a small patch of blue sky; by perceiving polarized light from it, they can keep their direction as surely as if they saw the sun itself.[2] This means of navigation only fails if the sky is clouded, since a clouded sky, unlike a blue sky, does not transmit polarized light. But if the sun is not behind a mountain, the bees can still do better than we can. For they can see the sun even through a thick cover of cloud that renders it quite invisible to us. Many an air or sea pilot might envy them this; but how it is done they have not yet revealed.

The process of learning in its relation to the "orientation flight"

A bee which has discovered food on a yellow background will learn to take her bearings from the yellow colour after a few visits.

It takes her about three seconds to approach the feeding

[1] The bee will certainly not see a thousand little spots of light separately or observe their changes. Just as in our consciousness the image received by each single cell of the retina from our *two* eyes is merged into a unified spatial picture, so the patterns seen by the bees' eyes must be changed in their brains into a relatively simple impression, though we can have no conception of what it is like.
[2] The experiments which show this form the first proof of the recognition of polarized light by bees, and are discussed on pp. 120 ff.

dish. While drinking the sugar-water the bee will remain over the colour for more than one minute. Finally she will rise into the air in a so-called orientation flight, circling round the feeding place in spirals of gradually increasing width. The importance of the period of sucking on top of the yellow colour, and particularly the importance of her "orientation flight", for memorizing the colour, seems quite obvious to an unbiassed observer. Yet he is wrong. This we can prove by the following simple experiment:

Three plates, painted white, blue, and yellow respectively, are placed on top of each other so that only the yellow plate is visible from above. We then cover this pile of plates with a glass sheet resting on cork feet (see fig. 34), which in its

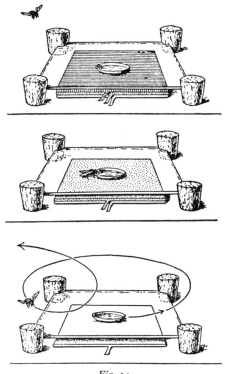

Fig. 34

turn supports a feeding-dish. To the first discoverer of this place the food appears to stand out against a yellow background. No sooner has she reached the feeding-dish than the yellow plate is removed, revealing the blue plate underneath. As a result, the bee is now feeding against a blue background. The moment she gets ready to start off again the blue plate is removed in its turn so that the departing bee while performing her "orientation flight" sees the feeding dish set out against a white background. On her return, however, she finds the dish restored to its former yellow background, then sucks on a blue background, starts off again from white, and so on in strict rotation. After this has been repeated a number of times, the three plates are set up *side by side*, during the temporary absence of the bee, and are then each provided with an empty dish. The visiting bee at once turns towards the *yellow* plate, in search of her food, ignoring the blue and the white plate. Of the three colours offered in turn she has memorized only the one which she had seen on her *approach* to the feeding place. Neither of the colours which she had seen during feeding or during her orientation flight had had the slightest influence on the result of her training. This holds good not only for colours but also for shapes which the bee has to memorize in connection with her food.

It would be wrong, though, to conclude from these experiments that the orientation flights performed by the bee on leaving a feeding place were of no importance whatever. It is during these orientation flights that the bees take their bearings from those more distant landmarks which help them to memorize the exact position of a certain spot. If a bee that has alighted on the feeding table at a certain point, A (see fig. 35) is taken, along with the dish from which she is drinking, and carried to point B, on leaving she will circle around this point in her orientation flight, and, more often than not, will return to B instead of returning to A for her next meal, which means that she will return to the point of her departure instead of to the place of her arrival.

Let us now apply our knowledge to conditions which are

more natural to the bee, e.g. to flower-visiting. A bee who approaches a source of nectar for the first time is sure to pay attention to the characteristic features of a newly discovered flower. It is not until she departs on her flight again that she will take notice of the characteristics of the surrounding country. The association formed with the food is much looser

Fig. 35

in the latter than in the former case where it is very close indeed. By this useful device the bee is led to spread her visits to a certain type of flower over a wide area instead of keeping too closely to the place of her first discovery, where the sources of nectar would all too soon be exhausted.

We now begin to understand why most bees, on leaving the hive for the first time, return to it after travelling a very short distance indeed. Unable to memorize the position of the hive except on her return, a beginner who, on her first outing, ventured too far afield, might not find her own home again.

CHAPTER ELEVEN

The Language of Bees

TRAINING experiments designed to throw light on the co-ordination of the bee's various sense organs have been repeatedly mentioned in previous chapters. One of the first conditions necessary for the success of such an experiment is that the trainees should make their appearance at the place where we intend to train them. To attract them to it, a simple device can be used: a few sheets of paper liberally smeared with honey are placed on the experimental table. It may take many hours or days even before a foraging worker appears; but once her attention is aroused by the smell of honey, she will soon regale herself greedily with the rich food. From now on we have an easy task, and we may start preparing our experiment, assured that not only will our first bee return to her food a few minutes later, but that dozens, nay hundreds, of newcomers will appear at our table within a few hours. If we try to trace their origin we shall find that almost without exception they came from the same colony as the first discoverer of the feeding-place. Hence it appears that in some way or other this first-comer must not only have announced her rich find to the other bees in the hive, but must also have led some of them out to it so that they might exploit it for themselves.

What we should like to know is *how* she did it. There is one way, and one way only, of obtaining a clear idea of the course of these events: this is actually to watch the behaviour of the returning bee as well as that of her companions who respond to her. This would not be feasible in an ordinary beehive but it can be done in a specially constructed observation hive of the type described on p. 34. By the side of such a hive we place a little dish filled with food. As soon as a visitor alights on it we mark her with paint (see p. 35) so as to be able to distinguish her from her companions amidst the bustle of the hive, and not lose sight of her again. In this way we shall see her coming in through the entrance hole, running up the combs, and presently stopping, to remain seated motionless for a short time, surrounded by her hive-mates. She then disgorges from her stomach all the honey she has just collected. This honey, which appears as a glistening droplet in her mouth, is immediately sucked up by two or three of her companions who face her with their tongues outstretched (see pl. xx). These are the bees who are responsible for disposing of the honey; they walk along the combs and, according to the colony's immediate needs, either feed their hungry companions or place the honey in the storage cells—internal matters these, with which the forager bee does not waste her time. While all these activities are going on, a drama is being enacted worthy of the pen of one of those great classical poets who have sung the praises of the bee. But, alas! it had not been discovered during their life-time. The kindly reader will therefore have to content himself with the following prosaic description.

A round dance as means of communication

The foraging bee, having got rid of her load, begins to perform a kind of "round dance". On the part of the comb where she is sitting she starts whirling around in a narrow circle, constantly changing her direction, turning now right, now left, dancing clockwise and anti-clockwise in quick succession, describing between one and two circles in each direction. This dance is performed among the thickest bustle of the hive. What makes it so particularly striking and attractive is the way it infects the surrounding bees; those sitting next to the dancer start tripping after her, always trying to keep their outstretched feelers in close contact with the tip of her abdomen. They take part in each of her manœuvrings

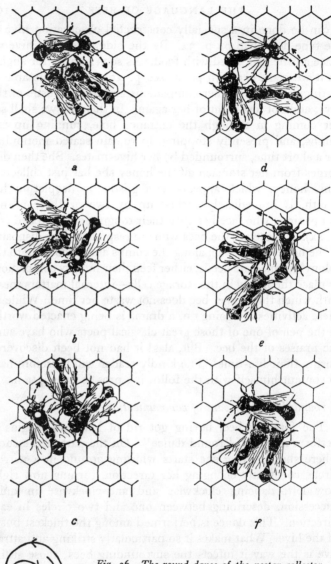

*Fig. 36. The round dance of the nectar collector.
The dancer (white spot) is followed by the other bees.*

so that the dancer herself, in her madly wheeling movements, appears to carry behind her a perpetual comet's tail of bees. In this way they keep whirling round and round, sometimes for a few seconds, sometimes for as long as half a minute, or even a full minute, before the dancer suddenly stops, breaking loose from her followers to disgorge a second or even a third droplet of honey while settling on one, or two other parts of the comb, each time concluding with a similar dance. This done, she hurries towards the entrance hole again to take off for her particular feeding-place, from where she is sure to bring back another load; the same performance being enacted at each subsequent return.

Under normal circumstances, the dance takes place in the darkness of a closed hive. Thus the dancer cannot be seen by her comrades. If they notice her behaviour and run after her every time she turns, they can only do so through their sense of feeling and smell.

What is the meaning of this round dance? One thing is obvious: it causes enormous excitement among the inmates of the hive sitting nearest to the dancers. Moreover, if we watch one of the bees in the dancer's train, we may actually see her preparing to depart, cleaning herself perfunctorily, then hurrying off in the direction of the entrance hole to leave the hive. In this case it is not long before the original discoverer of the feeding-place is joined there by the first newcomers. After returning with their loads, the new bees will dance in their turn; the greater the number of dancers, the greater will be the number of newcomers crowding around the feeding place. The relation between these two factors has now been established beyond any doubt: it is the dancing inside the hive that announces a rich find of food to the colony. But the problem that still remains unsolved is, how do the bees thus informed manage to find the *exact place* where the food is to be found?

The following explanation suggests itself: at the end of the dance, the bees informed by it might perhaps start rushing towards the entrance hole at the same time as the dancer, to fly after her on her next visit to the feeding-place. But this is definitely not the case. By keeping a close watch on the hive we may satisfy ourselves that no other bee ever keeps pace with the dancer during her hasty run over the combs towards the entrance hole; and, watching the dancer on her arrival at the feeding place, we may be equally sure that not a single bee has actually followed her in her flight. The arrival of newcomers at the feeding-place is sudden and unexpected, and quite independent of whether the honey has been replaced by a dish of pure sugar-water to avoid any attraction by scent. The method by which the position of the feeding place is communicated remained a mystery for quite a long time.

Then suddenly the mystery was solved in a very simple way in so far as targets situated near the hive were concerned. Suppose our feeding-place is situated at a distance of a little over ten yards to the south of the hive. Here, to a little dish of sugar-water, we manage to attract a group of about twelve bees which are marked immediately on their arrival. They go on collecting, and on their return to the hive they will each perform their dance on the combs. Next we place on the grass several glass dishes containing sugar-water, with a little honey added to make it easier for the bees to find them; these dishes are placed at a distance of about twenty yards, at all four points of the compass, north, south, east, and west of the hive. A few minutes after the first bees have started dancing, forager bees belonging to our colony will appear at *each* of the dishes. They do not know exactly where the dancers had been foraging; they just swarm out in all directions. There is such a crowd that at least some of them are bound to find the original feeding place almost at once, joining as newcomers those bees that had been marked before; while the rest discover the remaining dishes placed all round the hive. About the same number of bees will be found at each dish.

Hence a further question arises: how big is the area over which the search flights are extended?

In the following experiment, while retaining our first feed-

ing-place near the hive, we place the remaining feeding-dishes
further and further away. The greater the distance the longer
the time it will take the newcomers to find them. However,
even in our last experiment, with the little feeding-dish placed
at a distance of more than half a mile away in the middle of a
vast meadow, where it looked quite lost in the long grass,
and where it was separated from the hive by valleys as well
as by wooded hills, even there the bees arrived in the end, if
only in small numbers and after four hours' delay. All the
bees who settled on this dish were marked at once, and their
departure from the feeding place was then reported to the
people waiting at the hive by means of signals passed along a
chain of relays, so that before many minutes had passed we
knew that those bees had not just been chance visitors dropping
in from one of the neighbouring apiaries, but had been members of our observation hive that had been summoned by their
own dancers.

Suppose we remove the little sugar-water dish from our
feeding table, so that our marked bees find that there is no food
in the usual place? They will behave exactly as they would
if their natural food, the honey flow, had dried up owing to
bad weather, when their usual flowers temporarily cease to
provide them with nectar. The bees will stay at home, and
stop dancing. From then on the little honey dishes laid out
round the hive may have to wait on the lawn for hours or even
days on end before a single bee will visit them again.

This may surprise the reader who knows that those few
bees marked at our feeding-place are by no means the only
foragers in our colony. While they were frequenting our
sugar-water dishes, hundreds if not thousands of their hive
mates must have been foraging on various flowers, collecting
pollen as well as honey; and they must have gone on foraging
long after the flow of sugar-water at our artificial feeding place
had been suspended. Why have those other foragers on their
return from the flowers not aroused their companions by
dancing, and sent them off in their turn searching in all directions, so that among other things they would also find the

dishes? The answer is this: those who have found a *rich* source of nectar will certainly send their companions off to seek for food; not to sugar-water dishes, however, but to exactly the same sort of flowers that they themselves have just been successfully exploiting.

New light on the biological significance of flower scent

Flowers, not glass dishes, are the bee's natural drinking vessels. We shall come nearer to natural conditions by offering at our feeding site a little bunch of flowers, e.g. cyclamen, instead of our dish of sugar-water. To enable us to use any kind of flower we like for feeding purposes, regardless of how much nectar it happens to secrete at the time, each blossom is provided with a drop of sugar-water, replenished as soon as it is sucked up. So that the bees may go to the flowers only, and not pick up any sugar-water drops which may fall on the table, we stand the vase in a fairly large bowl of water (pl. xixa). The marked bees, finding a rich source of food provided for them by the cyclamen, will perform their usual dances on the combs.

In another place, selected at random, we arrange on the grass a bowl of cyclamen *without* any sugar-water, by the side of a bowl of flowers of a different kind, e.g. phlox (pl. xixb). Soon the alarm given by the dancers begins to have its effect: bees begin to appear all over the meadow, swarming about in their search for food. Having discovered our flower bowls, they make for the cyclamen, in which they bury themselves with a persistence suggesting that they are convinced that something is to be found there. But they pass by the bowl of phlox without taking the slightest interest in it.

Next, the cyclamen at our original feeding-site are replaced by phlox blossoms which in their turn have been richly doped with sugar-water. Now the same foragers, which not long ago had been busy on cyclamen, make for the phlox (pl. xixc). On the lawn our arrangement of vases, though itself unchanged, will provide a completely new picture within a few minutes: while interest in the cyclamen begins to slacken, the

XIX (a) Cyclamen vase standing in water

(b) A bowl of cyclamen and a bowl of phlox in the field not far from the feeding place in (a). The newcomers are only interested in the cyclamen

(c) Feeding bees on phlox

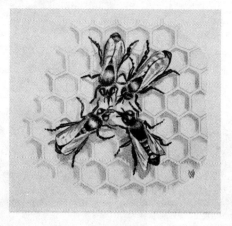

XX A returned forager (bottom left) giving nectar to three other bees

newcomers start visiting phlox, and what is more, we can see them flying into the neighbour's garden as well, where they busy themselves with all the phlox plants they can find. This is a strange sight for those who know that none but a butterfly's very long tongue can penetrate the deep floral tubes of the phlox blossoms. The bee, with her short proboscis, is quite unable to reach the nectar hidden deep down in the flower and is therefore normally not seen on phlox. Obviously the foraging bees know exactly what to look for, which means that the dancers inside the hive must have told them exactly what sort of flower had offered them so rich a reward.

The experiment described here is sure to be successful; no matter whether the food is offered on cyclamen or phlox, on gentian or vetch, thistle blossom or ranunculus, beans or immortelles. If we consider the conditions prevailing in nature we soon realize how appropriate this behaviour is on the part of the bee: whenever a plant newly come into flower is discovered by the scout bees, they announce their discovery by means of a dance; their companions thus aroused are then able to go straight to the flowers whose rich nectar secretion had provoked the dancing, instead of wasting their time fruitlessly seeking among flowers which may have nothing to offer. But how is this behaviour to be explained?

It is unbelievable that the bee language should possess a separate expression for every variety of flower. Yet such is the case. Revealed to us here is a language of flowers in the true sense of the word—incredibly simple, charming, and well-designed for its purpose. While the forager-bee is sucking the sweet juice out of a flower, a trace of its scent adheres to her body. While dancing on her return she still carries this scent. Her companions who trip after her briskly examining her with their feelers—which act as their organs of smell—are able to perceive it. They commit it to memory and then go out in search of it, swarming all over the place in consequence of this latest "alarm".

We can make this relation even more evident if we replace our natural flowers by essential oils or by an artificial scent.

For example, we may feed marked bees from a glass dish placed on a base scented with peppermint oil. As soon as these bees have started dancing, the newcomers swarming out from the hive will approach and visit any object that has been made to smell of peppermint, while all other scents are ignored. Whenever we change the odour prevailing at the feeding-place the bees will change the goal of their search accordingly.

However, in our original arrangement (see p. 45), in which the bees are fed from an unscented glass dish, there is no specific scent adhering to them which the hive-mates following the dancers can recognize. Even in this case they do not leave their hive without any clue, though the one they have is negative: whenever they encounter scented flowers on their flight they realize that these cannot be among the food sources to be searched for, and consequently they do not waste their time on them. Instead they go on searching in places where there is no flower scent to be perceived as did those bees which appeared at our various glass dishes on the lawn.

Early plant biologists thought of the flower scent as nothing but a means of attracting insects in search of food. As far as bees are concerned it is, in addition, the clue by which they recognize the kind of flower they happen to have successfully visited, as opposed to all other flowers of a similar colour. This discrimination is essential for the formation of that "flower constancy" that is known to exist in bees (see p. 45). But flower scent has an importance far beyond this. The returning forager bee, not content with summoning her companions to fly out in search of food by her dancing, describes what they are to look for by means of the specific flower scent carried on her body, in such a simple but unmistakable way that the most precise expressions of any word language could not better it.

How the flower scent is brought home

A casual observer might describe certain flowers as "scentless". Indeed, a yellow ranunculus, a blue gentian, or for that matter a scarlet runner, though they shine like beacons, do not fill our rooms with any kind of fragrance. Yet unless our organs of smell are completely dulled by excessive smoking, we can distinguish a delicate scent in each of these flowers if a bunch of about a dozen or so is held up close to our nostrils.

Among the many flowers pollinated by insects, scentless ones, like bilberry or Virginia creeper, are rare exceptions. As we would expect, bees foraging on any of these flowers do not convey any information to their colonies about the goals to be sought for. It is all the more surprising to learn that the very faintest flower scent, only just noticeable to us, suffices to reveal the exact location of the dancer's foraging place to her companions inside the hive. How is it possible for such a delicate fragrance to remain perceptible after having been carried all the way home by a foraging bee?

Part of the explanation lies in the fact that odorous substances adhere to the body of a bee more strongly than to most other objects. If we impregnate the following objects with the scent of a flower: pieces of glass, china, and various metals, little balls of paper or cotton wool, dead bodies of bees and other insects, we shall find that it adheres best to the body of the honey-bee. We can check this with our own noses. It is the bee herself, however, who provides the most relevant answer to our question. If bees that have been trained to seek for a certain flower scent are confronted with a number of objects, among them bees' bodies which have first been exposed to the same scent and then to the air for some time, they will perceive the scent on the bee's body long after they have ceased to recognize it on any of the other objects. The surface of that body seems to be particularly well-equipped by nature for retaining scent. However, yet another factor has to be considered. The nectar secreted at the bottom of a flower is contained within the fragrant corolla, where it becomes saturated with a specific flower scent. The foraging bee, after sucking it up, carries a sample of this scent home along with the nectar. Once she has arrived at the hive, she conveys this

scent to the bees surrounding her, through the act of feeding
them with the sugary juice. Among these bees are her dancing
partners who take off in search of food as soon as they have
received the password in the form of scent from the dancer's
mouth.

The truth of this has been confirmed by the following
experiment: some sugar-water dropped into blossoms of phlox
was left standing until it had become saturated with their
scent. The phlox-scented sugar-water was then offered to

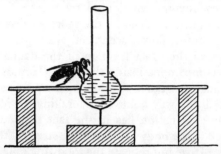

*Fig. 37.   The bee sucks sugar-water scented with phlox through a narrow gap
in such a way that no scent adheres to her body.*

the bees in such a way that they had to suck it up through a
narrow crack without ever exposing their bodies to the odour
(fig. 37). The bees dancing on their return fed their companions with the scented sugar solution. In order to judge
the effect of this feeding, we had again to watch the behaviour
of our bees at the site, where the two bowls, one filled with
phlox and the other with cyclamen, stood on the lawn side by
side, not far from our first feeding place (see pl. xxb). The
newcomers starting from the hive alighted only on phlox.
They selected it just as distinctly and unmistakably in another
experiment, in which the forager-bees were made to sit on
phlox blossoms while sucking up perfectly *scentless* sugar-
water through a narrow cleft. This shows that the scent
carried by the bee in her honey-stomach, and the scent
adhering to her body, will *both* have an effect on the bees surrounding the dancer in the hive. By causing bees to suck up

phlox-scented sugar-water through a narrow cleft while they sat on the blossoms of cyclamen (fig. 38) we made the two factors compete with one another. We then noticed at our observation site that twice as many bees alighted on the phlox bowl as on the cyclamen bowl. In a test in which conditions were reversed, bees sitting on phlox blossoms were made to drink sugar-water saturated with cylamen scent. Of the two bowls standing side by side, the one with cyclamen was now

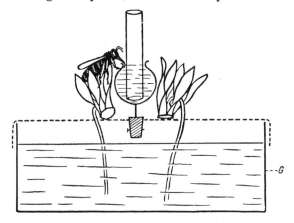

Fig. 38. The bee sucks sugar-water scented with phlox through the gap, while her body takes on the scent of cyclamen.

G, glass dish with water covered over with wire netting.

visited twice as often by newcomers as the one with phlox. From this we concluded that the flower scent absorbed in the nectar solution which is carried home in the bee's honey-stomach is of greater consequence than that carried externally. It will easily carry the day when the food source is a long way from the beehive. The same experiment was repeated with a distance of over six hundred yards between the hive and the feeding place. So long a flight involved so much exposure to the air that the scent adhering to the bee's body was bound to lose much of its intensity. And in fact, newcomers arriving from the hive were now exclusively guided by the scent that had been transported in the dancer's honey-stomach.

This account shows the great biological importance of the
flower scent which adheres to the nectar and is carried home,
as if in well-sealed little bottles, in the honey-stomachs of the
bees.

The balance of supply and demand

The biological importance of the bees' dances is above all
due to the fact that they can be evoked only by a good, plentiful food source. Unless a honey crop is really abundant enough
to justify the calling up of a large army of foragers, no dances
are performed inside the hive. The following gives a good
instance of this.

We cut fresh acacia twigs, and put them in a bowl of
water in a place to which no insects had access; an abundant
nectar crop accumulated in their blossoms within a few hours.
A bunch of such twigs was then offered to the bees at their
usual feeding place. By means of a little trick we made them
approach this new source of food at once. As soon as they
arrived the bees proceeded to exploit this rich natural crop.
After drinking their fill they flew home to dance, summoning
reinforcements from the hive. Soon there were so many of
them that the nectar sucked up by the foragers could no longer
be replenished by the flowers themselves at the required
speed: the formerly abundant crop had become a scanty one.
Foraging went on with undiminished zeal, but dancing ceased
altogether. Consequently no newcomers from the hive came
to swell the numbers of foraging bees.

The richness of a nectar crop consists for bees not only in
its quantity, but also in the degree of its sweetness. If we
drop several lumps of sugar into a glass of water one a ter
another, there comes a moment when, in spite of continuo is
stirring, we wait in vain for the last lump to be dissolve l.
This last and any further lumps will only fall to pieces and
form solid dregs on the bottom of the glass. We have dissolved as much sweetness as the water can hold in solution.
In other words we have produced a "saturated" sugar solution. We find a similar saturated solution as nectar in certain

flowers. Obviously it is worth summoning all possible forces in order to bring in as much of such a syrup as the stomach of each bee can hold.

Other kinds of plants produce a weaker nectar, poorer in sugar and therefore lacking in sweetness. The bees collecting it bring home a much smaller amount of sugar for every load of liquid than those foraging from the more concentrated nectar. To call vigorously for reinforcements would not be as expedient for them as it was in the other case, and they do not in fact do so. As the sweetness of the nectar decreases, so does the vigour of the dances; the less ardently the dances are performed the less persuasive is their effect.

However abundant the nectar, the bees will stop dancing altogether as soon as its sugar content falls below a certain level. We thus see that by means of a very simple device the number of foragers summoned to work each crop is increased or reduced in strict proportion to its yield. Plants which produce a nectar superior both in sweetness and in abundance, will receive the greatest number of visitors, because the bees who have discovered them will dance with greater vigour than the bees who may have found an inferior crop available at the same time somewhere else. The specific scent carried home by the dancing bees in each case guarantees the success of this "summons by degree". A bee is able to say accurately and firmly: "Today the richest crop is to be found where there is plum-blossom scent". In this way she is able to ensure that nectar flowing from the best and most prolific food source eventually reaches a very great number of honey cells in preference to other types of food. At the same time the plants which produce the largest quantity of the sweetest nectar get the briskest traffic of bees. This, in turn, ensures pollination of the largest number of flowers and consequently the most abundant production of seed.

The bee's scent bottle

Previously, in each of our experiments, we have been using only one feeding-place at a time. This time we fed the bees

from our observation hive at two different feeding-places, so
that one group of marked bees was being fed at one place A,
to the left of the hive, while at the same time a second group

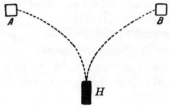

was feeding at a place B to the
right of the hive. There was
no intermingling between the
two groups (see fig. 39). We
then offered an "abundant
crop"—a dish filled with sugar-
water—at A, while the bees

Fig. 39. H, *beehive.* A *and* B, *two* feeding at B got a "scanty
feeding-places. crop" in the form of blotting

paper soaked with the same syrup. Whereas members of this
latter group went on foraging without ever making an attempt
to dance, the bees fed at A of course performed their usual
dances on their arrival at the hive.

The dancers started off their companions on an all-round
search. As neither of the feeding-places had been provided with a scent, newcomers looked out for a scentless goal.
They were likely to pass B just as often as A during their
search, and might join one of the groups foraging there if they
felt like it. As a result we would have expected an equal number of foragers to appear in both places. However, we were
surprised to see that after a certain lapse of time the number
of newcomers appearing at A increased to ten times the number of those appearing at B, where the crop was poorer.
Doubtless such behaviour is advantageous to the bee. At the
same time it proved that there must still be a "word" of the
bee language that we had not yet discovered. For how are the
bees visiting the "scanty crop" to know that it would pay
them better to fly somewhere else?

After further close observation, it was the behaviour of bees
foraging in both places which provided the missing clue: this
was another word of a "scent language", except for the fact
that this time the scent was produced by the bee herself
instead of being conveyed to her from a flower. Every
worker-bee carries her own little scent bottle along ready for

use. This scent organ, which we mentioned above (p. 92), consists of a little fold of skin near the tip of the tail, normally invisible, but which can be turned inside out at will in the form of a damp, glistening pad. In this way it can release and disseminate a scent secreted by special glands with which this pocket is lined. It has been proved by experiment that for bees this scent is extremely strong and they can recognize it from a great distance. The bee is, of course, particularly sensitive to the body smell of her fellows, and this smell can even be detected by human begins.

On approaching the well-filled feeding-dish the bees turn their scent pockets inside out, and before alighting on it keep buzzing round it for some time, thus impregnating the air with their scent pads, which can sometimes be seen protruding even after they have started to feed. By doing this they attract towards a profitable food source every single bee that happens to be flying about in search of food, often from a considerable distance. On the other hand, the bees who have been foraging at a scanty crop keep their scent organs closed away inside their little pockets (see pl. xxɪa).

We have mentioned before that ten times as many recruits appeared at the rich crop as visited the poor one. We proved that it was the lure of the bee scent, and nothing else, that was responsible for this enormous difference. We fed the bees again at both A and B, this time offering a "rich crop", a dish well filled with sugar-water at both places. We varied the conditions, however, by applying, with a fine brush, a thin film of shellac to the openings of the scent pockets of the bees frequenting place B, which prevented the scent pads from functioning. The bees did not mind this, if indeed they noticed it at all. At any rate they behaved like the bees of group A in every way except that they could not disseminate any scent. Though both groups performed their dances on the combs as usual, and though both had been offered rich crops frequented by their foragers in exactly the same way, yet the number of newcomers was ten times greater at A, where the scent organs of the bees had been working, than at

B, where the scent organs of the foragers had been put out of action.

We may take it for granted that whenever the bee visits real flowers, her scent organs play a similar part.

The "wagging dance" tells the distance of the food supply

For many years we carried on experiments with the feeding-place set up close to the hive. Accordingly it did not strike us as peculiar that, in the tests which followed each training, newcomers swarming out from the hive arrived at the place near the hive earlier and in greater numbers than they did at, places which were farther off. There came a day, however, when we moved our feeding-place to a site several hundred yards from the hive. The number of newcomers to be seen searching near the hive immediately diminished; but large numbers of them kept arriving at the distant feeding-place. For the first time we began to suspect that the dancing might reveal, among other things, the distance that the foragers had to cover.

If bees from our observation hive are trained in such a way that one group of marked insects collects food from a place near the hive, while a second group, differently marked, collects it from a more distant place, we see this astonishing scene being enacted on the combs: while all the bees belonging to the first group perform their usual round dances (see fig. 36), those belonging to the second group perform what I have called "wagging dances" (*Schwänzeltänze*). In these dances the bee runs along a narrow semi-circle, makes a sharp turn, and then runs back in a straight line to her starting point. Next she describes another semi-circle, this time in the opposite direction, thus completing a full circle, once more returning to her starting point in a straight line. She does this for several minutes, remaining on the same spot all the time: semi-circle to the left, straight back, then semi-circle to the right, straight back, and so on indefinitely. The characteristic feature which distinguishes this "wagging dance" from the "round dance" is a very striking, rapid wagging of the bee's abdomen performed only during her straight run (fig. 40 and pl. xxib). This wagging dance commands just as much attention among the bees tripping behind the dancer as does the round dance.

If our feeding-place is gradually moved from a place close to the hive to one further away from it, the round dance will

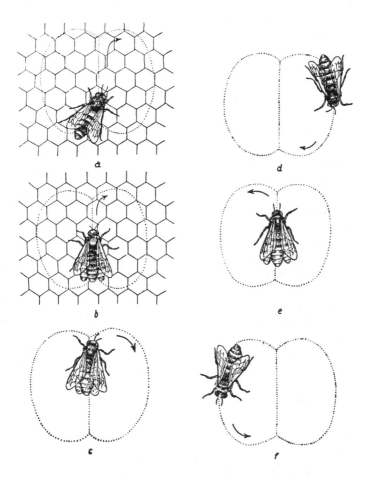

Fig. 40. *The wagging dance*

begin to merge into a wagging dance when a distance of between fifty and one hundred yards is reached. If, on the other hand, we start at a distant feeding-place and move it step by step towards the hive, then the wagging dance will give way to a round dance, again at approximately the same distance. The round dance and the wagging dance represent two different words of the bee language: the round dance indicates the presence of a food source fairly near the hive, and the wagging dance points to one further afield. That this meaning is understood by the inmates of the hive was proved by experiment.[1]

We know that the bee's range of flight extends two or three miles all round the hive. Therefore the knowledge that food was to be found either "less than a hundred yards away" or "more than a hundred yards away" from the hive would not in itself be very helpful. When in a new series of experiments we began to move the feeding-place in very small steps towards the outer boundary of the bee's range of flight, we finally discovered the law ruling the performance of the wagging dance, a law that enables bees as well as men to derive from observation of the dance much more precise information than could have been anticipated. It is this:

With a distance of a hundred yards between hive and feeding-place, the dances are hastily performed, the separate turns following each other in quick succession (see fig. 41). But as the distance of the food supply increases these turns follow each other at longer and longer intervals, making the dances appear more and more stately, the straight waggle run at the same time gradually becoming more prolonged and more vigorous. Using a stop-watch we found that the bee travels along the straight part of the waggle run between nine and ten times in a quarter of a minute if the distance between the

---

[1] In earlier, German, editions of this book the wagging dance was wrongly described as the dance of the pollen-collecting bees. This was due to the fact that we had only been watching pollen-collectors, which had been foraging among natural crops growing at some distance from our hive, whereas we had happened always to offer our sugar-water at a site near the hive. Hence we got the impression that round dances indicated the presence of nectar, while wagging dances announced the presence of pollen.

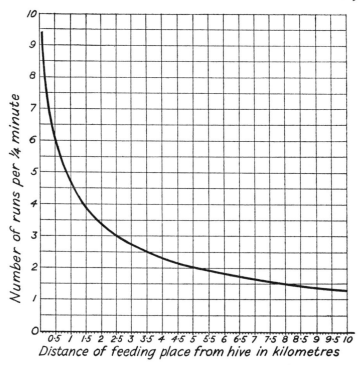

Fig. 41.   *The curve shows how the tempo of the dance decreases with increasing distance.*

hive and the feeding-place is a hundred metres, six times at a distance of five hundred metres, four to five times at a distance of a thousand metres, twice at five thousand, and barely more than once at a distance of ten thousand metres (fig. 41). The agreement between measurements taken on different days, in different years, or even with different colonies, is simply amazing. This is all the more remarkable as the bees do not carry watches. Obviously they must possess a very acute sense of time, enabling the dancer to move in the rhythm appropriate to the occasion, and her companions to comprehend and interpret her movements correctly. Can they really do all this? And how accurately do the newcomers

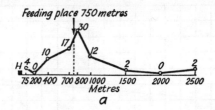

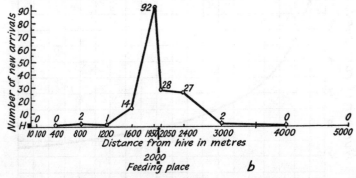

Fig. 42.   Results of two distance experiments.

(a) *Feeding-place at which bees were marked, 750 metres from hive.*
(b) *Feeding-place 2,000 metres from hive.*
The figures on the curves give the numbers of new arrivals.

keep to the distance indicated to them by the wagging dance?
In order to discover this, several numbered bees were fed with
sugar-water to which a little lavender scent had been added,
at a definite distance from the hive; similarly scented bait, but
no food, was placed at other, varying, distances. The foragers
danced on the combs, sending their comrades to look for the
source of the lavender scent. During this experiment, the
feeding-place was 750 metres away from the hive; scented
boards without food were placed in the same direction at
regular intervals of 75, 200, 400, 700, 800, 1,000, 1,500,
2,000, and 2,500 metres. An observer sat at each of these
points, noting each bee that flew there in the course of an hour
and a half. The numbers of new bees arriving at the different

points are registered in fig. 42a; the curve shows the result. In another test, the feeding-place was 2,000 metres from the hive and the scented bait lay at distances of 100, 400, 800, 1,200, 1,600, 1,950, 2,050, 2,400, 3,000, 4,000, and 5,000[1] metres (fig. 42b). The bees, which had been notified by the dance, followed its indication beyond all expectation, persistently searching by the hour at the correct distances.

How do they know at all how far they have flown? Let us take a look at their measuring system in windy weather. If they encounter a head wind on their flight to the feeding-place, on their return they indicate a greater distance than if there had been no wind; with a following wind, a shorter distance is indicated. If there is no wind and they have to fly up a steep hillside to reach the feeding-place, the dance is affected as though the distance were longer; if the flight is downhill, the effect on the dance is as though the distance were shorter. It seems, therefore, that their calculation of distance depends on the time required or the strength exerted.

The wagging dance also indicates the direction of the food supply

It would be of little use to the bees if they knew that a lime-tree was in full flower a mile away from the hive if at the same time they were ignorant of its direction. In fact, the wagging dance gives them this information as well. It is contained in the direction of the "wagging" runs during the figure of the dance.

For showing the right direction, bees use two different methods, depending on whether the dance takes place (as it usually does) inside the hive on the *vertical* comb or outside on the *horizontal* platform. Direction-finding from a horizontal surface is probably older in the history of the bee folk. It is also easier to understand, so we shall begin with it. It should be remembered that the sun is used as a compass (p. 93, ff.). When the foraging bee flies from the hive to the feeding-place with the sun at an angle of 40° to the left

[1] Bees only fly to these distant feeding places if they seem very tempting and nothing good can be found nearer to hand.

and in front of her, she keeps this angle in her wagging dance
and thus indicates the direction of the feeding-place (fig. 43).
The bees who follow after the dancer notice their own position with respect to the sun while following the wagging
dance; by maintaining the same position on their flight, they
obtain the direction of the feeding-source. This applies only
if the dancer can see the sun—or at least blue sky (see pp. 81
ff. and p. 96)—for instance during a dance on the alighting
board. This takes place quite frequently when some of the

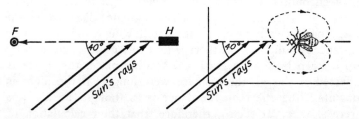

Fig. 43. *Giving the sun's bearing in a wagging dance on a horizontal surface.*
Left: H, *hive.* F, *feeding-place. Right: wagging dance on a horizontal surface.*
- - -, direction of flight to feeding-place.

inmates of the hive await the homecoming foragers outside
on the board during warm weather. One can also take a comb
out of the hive and hold it in a horizontal position in mid-air.
The dancers are not easily fooled. They point in the direction in which they have been foraging, and if we rotate the
horizontal comb like a railway turntable, they allow the dance
floor to turn under their feet and keep their direction like a
compass needle. But if we hide the sky from their eyes, they
dance at random and become completely disorientated.

Inside the hive it is dark, the sky is invisible; besides, the
comb surfaces stand upright and so an indication of direction
in the way we have just described is impossible. Under these
circumstances the bees use the second method, a very remarkable one. Instead of using the horizontal angle with the sun,
which they followed during their flight to the feeding-place,
they indicate direction by means of gravity, in the following
way: upward wagging runs mean that the feeding-place lies

towards the sun; downward wagging runs indicate the opposite direction; upward wagging runs 60° to the left of the vertical point to a source of food 60° to the left of the direction of the sun (fig. 44) and so on. Experience gained by the newcomers in this way, in the darkness of the hive, by means of

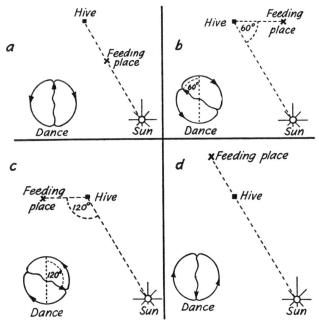

Fig. 44. *Giving the sun's bearing in a dance on a vertical comb surface. The little diagrams on the left of each drawing show the dance as it appears on the vertical comb.*

their delicate sense of feeling for gravity is transferred to a bearing on the sun once they are outside the hive.

Just as we discovered from the "step experiment" whether the instructions about distance had been followed, so now we shall see by the "fan experiment" whether the bees really fly in the direction they have been given. Fig. 45 shows the results of such an experiment. A few numbered bees were fed on a scented foundation F, 250 yards away from the hive.

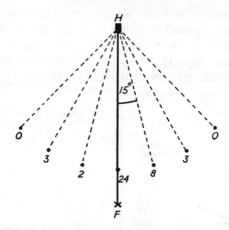

Fig. 45. The results of a "fan" experiment: H, hive. F, feeding-place. The black dots represent scented bait without food, the numbers by each one indicate the number of bees that arrived at each point.

Similar scented objects, this time without food, were arranged in the shape of a fan at angles of 15° from the hive and at a distance of 200 yards from it. The numbers in the diagram indicate the number of newcomers that arrived at the observation points during a test period of 1½ hours. Only a few of the bees deviated from the right path.

In mountainous country even flying creatures cannot always reach their objective by the most direct route. By what means will the bees show their hive-mates how to reach a source of food by an indirect route? There was plenty of opportunity to answer this question in the mountainous country near the Wolfgangsee. One day our observation hive was placed behind a ridge of rock on the Schafberg; a quickly-made feeding-place with numbered bees was set out at the foot of a cliff, indicated by a cross in pl. xxiib. The sketch in fig. 46 shows a plan of the positions and distances in the area of the experiment. The foragers flew up and down along the track marked by two sides of the acute-angled triangle, but in their dances they indicated the direction neither of the take-off from the hive nor of the second part of the route to the objective—as in both

XXI (a) *Three bees at the feeding dish; the bee on the left has pushed out* **her**
scent organ, which can be seen as a small, shining pad just under **the**
hindmost part of her abdomen (under the X). *The bee on the right has*
pulled in her scent organ

(b) *The tail-wagging dance*

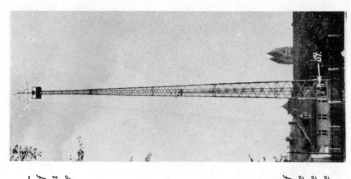

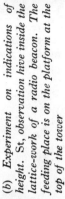

b

XXII

(a) Scene of the 'indirect route' experiment on the Schafberg. X position of the feeding place. The observation hive is on the other side of the ridge of rock at roughly the same height

(b) Experiment on indications of height. St, observation hive inside the lattice-work of a radio beacon. The feeding place is on the platform at the top of the tower

a

cases they would have confused their fellows. The wagging
run indicated the 'bee-line' to the feeding-place, although
actually they never flew along it. This was the only way
they could guide their fellows to the right place; the latter
flew in the direction shown for a limited period, since they
knew from the dances what the correct *distance* should be
and so they found their objective even with the detour.

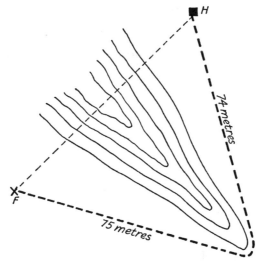

Fig. 46.   *Sketch of the "indirect route" experiment on the Schafberg.* H, hive.
F, *feeding-place.* — — — — *course taken.* - - - - - - *direct line to object.*

The behaviour of the guides was thus adjusted to the situation and was completely sensible. That they are able to
fly by an indirect route and yet reconstruct the true direction
without the aid of ruler, protractor, or drawing-board, is one
of the most wonderful accomplishments in the life of the bee
and indeed in all creation.

It might almost be imagined that they could find a solution
to any task however difficult. But in *one* case they failed.
The hive stood inside the lattice work of a radio beacon
(pl. xxiib). The feeding-place was attached to the end of a
rope swinging in the wind and was pulled up to the top of the

beacon by a winch, thus being directly above the entrance hole of the hive. The bees have no word for "up" in their language. There are no flowers in the clouds. The foragers on the feeding-table at the top of the beacon did not know what direction to indicate and did only round dances. Their comrades down below searched in all directions and flew up and down the meadow, but not one of them found the source of food. When the feeding-place was placed on the grass at a distance from the hive corresponding with the height of the tower, the indication of direction worked perfectly.

Both the wagging dance, with its direction-giving run, and the round dance with its circular motion, show them how to proceed with surprising clearness; one tells them to hurry into the far distance, the other makes them search round the hive. By a well-regulated system those who are to seek far afield are given precise indications of the object of their journey. But when hundreds of newcomers start out on a journey there are usually some who do not conform; a few search far afield after a round dance (p. 105) or near at hand after a wagging dance (p. 120, fig. 42), or in the wrong direction. Have they misunderstood the language? Or are they stubborn nonconformists who prefer to go their own way? Whatever the cause of this "wrong" action may be, these eccentrics also have their use. Suppose a field of rape is flowering in the south, it is obviously a good thing to direct the inhabitants of the hive towards it as quickly as possible, but at the same time it is worth investigating whether there is not a similar field in flower somewhere else. Thanks to the eccentrics who do not follow the rules, all possible sources of food are quickly brought to the notice of the bees.

The dances of the pollen collectors

As the second foodstuff indispensable for the life of the colony, pollen is also collected by honey-bees. Pollen collectors too will perform the kind of dances that tell their hive mates where an abundant crop is to be found. If the pollen crop is close to the hive, they will perform a round dance, if the crops are more distant, wagging dances are performed that obey the same rules about distances and direction-giving as do the wagging dances of the nectar gatherers.

There is a slight difference, however: nectar collectors pass on information as to the kind of flower visited by means of the scent which remains on their bodies and permeates the honey stomach (pp. 108 ff.). The pollen collectors carry no scented nectar home, but they bring with them, in the pollen, an actual particle of the flower they have visited. Pollen has its own specific scent, quite distinct from the scent of petals, and again different for each type of flower. In this case the pollen "breeches" are the carriers of scent. This can be proved by the following experiment:

Two separate feeding-places were set up for our pollen collectors. While one group of individually-marked bees was made to forage on wild roses in the first, a second group collected the pollen of a large campanula species in the other. Then we removed both crops to stop the feeding altogether.

It was not long before our foragers, having looked for their food in vain, decided to stay at home, except for a few solitary scouting bees visiting one of the old feeding-places occasionally in order to find out whether the food had reappeared. As soon as fresh campanula flowers were set up at the familiar site

Fig. 47. H, *hive*. R, *feeding-place with roses*. C, *feeding-place with campanula*.

the first scout bee to discover them at once collected their pollen, returned, and then danced in the hive. The first bees to respond to this dance after their interval of fasting were members of the campanula scent group. At once they rushed off towards the familiar feeding-place to take up their foraging where they had left off. Soon the dances were in full swing again, attracting more and still more newcomers. There was no foraging for the rose collectors this time: they stayed at home, remembering that campanula scent was none of their concern.

The result of this experiment has still not taught us whether the scent that prompted the behaviour of the bees was that of the petals or of the pollen of campanula. In order to decide this question we offered our bees, in a modification of our first experiment, after the fasting interval, a bunch of campanula flowers whose stamens had been replaced by those of roses (see fig. 48). A scout bee arrived at the familiar site

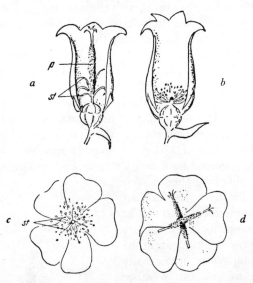

Fig. 48. (a) *Bloom of* Campanula medium, *a part of the corolla having been removed to show the inside; the pollen on the pushed-back stamens remains mostly clinging to the pistil.* (b) *Bloom of the same flower after removal of the pollen-carrying parts which are replaced by the stamens of a rose.* (c) *Flower of a rose,* Rosa moschata. (d) *Rose flower after the removal of its own stamens with two pistils holding pollen of Campanula.* st, stamens. p, pistil.

and finding that campanula flowers had been restored to it soon burrowed into one of the corollae to gather its pollen. Here we had a situation in which a member of the campanula group, foraging at the familiar campanula place, had been made to collect rose pollen from a campanula. She returned to the hive, danced, and her colleagues, who for hours and days had been foraging on campanula like her, took not the slightest notice of her lively performance. It was the rose collectors who, though not personally acquainted with her, came rushing over to the dancer to take a sniff at her "breeches".

After that they dashed out of the entrance hole, expecting to find fresh rose blossoms at *their* familiar (rose) feeding-place, for which they looked, of course, in vain. In thus allowing themselves to be fooled, the bees had told us their secret: we now knew that their actions were decided by the scent of the rose pollen they had brought in, and not that of the petals of the campanula corolla they had crawled into.

The same experiment can be carried out the other way round with corresponding results: a scout bee of the rose group who has found campanula pollen inside rose blossoms arouses, with her dances, pollen collectors belonging to the campanula and not to the rose group of foragers.

A hinged beehive and an experiment on the perception of polarized light.

In order to study the behaviour of bees on a horizontal dance-floor more precisely, an observation hive which can be tilted is used. By turning a screw it can be fixed in any desired sloping position. If the surface of the combs slant at an angle of only about 15° (pl. xxiiia), the dancers can still indicate a bearing on the sun by means of an upward wagging run. Each angle between the feeding-place and the position of the sun is indicated by a corresponding angle from the line which gives the steepest slope towards the top of the slanting surface. Apparently they have a very strong sense of gravity.

But if the comb lies in a completely horizontal position, they cannot run upwards on it, and the method discussed on p. 122 (fig. 44) for direction-finding no longer applies. It is an amusing sight to see the bees continuing to dance with undiminished vigour under such circumstances—so long as the sky is invisible to them—but with an absolutely aimless wagging run, which constantly changes direction in a haphazard way. As soon as the dancers are shown the sun or a patch of blue sky, the dances become orientated and point directly towards the feeding-place.

It has already been said that this astonishing method of taking their bearing from the blue sky is to be attributed to their perception of polarized light (pp. 95 ff.)   We shall now discuss how this can be proved.

Plate xxiiib shows the observation hive in a horizontal position. The glass disc over the comb is covered with a board in which a square window has been cut; over it lies a large polarizing filter in a circular frame which can be rotated (p. 82 ff.).   In this experiment the hive is shut in on three sides; the dancers on the comb can only see a small patch of blue sky (for example to the north) through the window in the board and hence through the polarizing filter. The light from the sky is partly polarized and has, as we already know (p. 96), a different vibration for each point of the compass. The polarizing filter is in this respect even more thorough and makes *all* the light rays that pass through it vibrate in one direction only. If we now put the movable filter that is above the dancing bees in such a position that the rays of light coming through it keep the direction of vibration that they have in the northern sky at that moment, the bees continue to dance in the right way and point towards the feeding place. But if the filter is turned so that the vibration of the polarized light is altered, then the bees too change direction and point wrongly. The extent to which they go wrong does not necessarily correspond with the angle through which the filter was turned.

The amount of deviation, and the fact that this deviation was really caused by the rays of polarized light, can be determined by making use of the star-shaped filters described on p. 83, fig. 29. It may be assumed to correspond with the view of one single *ommatidium* from the compound eye of the bee; if the sky is observed through a star-shaped filter, an effect is produced similar to that obtained through the bee's eye. An experiment will make this clear.

A few numbered bees from the horizontal observation hive collect sugar-water from a feeding-place situated due west. A

XXIII (a) The hinged observation hive in a tilted position. Even on such a slight slope the bees can still follow the direction of gravity in the dance

(b) The observation hive in the horizontal position, covered with the movable polarizing filter

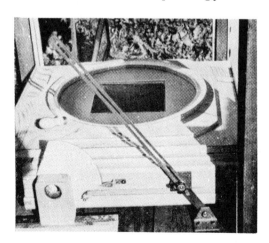

patch of blue sky in the west, and so in the direction of the feeding-place, is uncovered for the dancers. Their wagging runs point towards the west. Now the large round filter is so arranged that vibrations of light coming from the western sky remain unaltered. The bees continue to dance in the correct manner. Their dance is obviously adapted to the pattern of the vibrations of polarized light characteristic of the western sky. This pattern we can see ourselves if the western sky is viewed through the star-shaped filter. On their flight to the feeding-place the bees see this pattern *in front* of them. In consequence they point towards the west (we can forget M2 in fig. 49a for the moment). Now, however, the filter above the hive is turned 30° away from its original position. Immediately the direction of the dance is changed and the bees point 35° to the south of west. We see through the star-shaped filter—an artificial bee-eye, as it were—the

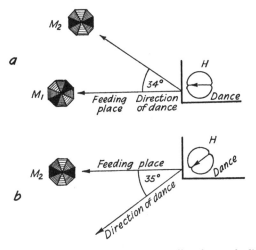

Fig. 49. (a) *Bees from the observation hive* H *collect from a feeding-place in the west. If they are given a free view of the western sky during their dance on the horizontal comb, they point correctly to the west. In the wagging-dance they orientate themselves according to the pattern* M1 *which is in front of them during their flight to the feeding-place.* (b) *By placing a polarizing filter in front, the pattern* M1 *is changed into pattern* M2 *for the dancers. They point in a wrong direction because they see pattern* M2 *in front of them* 34° *to the right, during their flight to the feeding-place.*

pattern M1 in the western sky. If another polarizing filter is held in front of the star-shaped filter, pointing the same way as the filter above the hive, then the pattern M1 changes into the pattern M2. The same effect is presumed to be produced in the bee's eye. If we look up into the sky through the artificial eye after removing the front filter, then the pattern M2 appears in one place only, 34° north of west. In their flight from the hive to the feeding-place, the bees saw the pattern M1 exactly in front of them, and the pattern M2 34° in front of them to the right (fig. 49a). They flew directly towards M1 keeping 34° to the left of M2. In the experiment, they were shown M2 in the west, that is shifted 34° to the left. They saw nothing else but this pattern. Their dance was thus orientated accordingly and they pointed 35° to the left of this pattern, as in their flight to the feeding-place—with an error of only 1°.

Naturally one such experiment does not afford certain proof. But as essentially the same results were obtained in about one hundred differently modified experiments, we can be certain that bees take their bearings from polarized light from the sky.

Dances in the swarm cluster

Preoccupation over obtaining sufficient food is by no means the only affair in the life of bees which depends on mutual communication. Of other such activities, however, as yet we know but one: the choosing of a home by the bee swarm.

Immediately after swarming the bees gather round their queen in a formation which looks like a bunch of grapes hanging from a tree (pl. ix, facing p. 28). It is now up to the scouts to find suitable accommodation for the new colony: in a hollow tree, a cave, or hole in a wall, or in an empty hive, and so on. Dozens of scouts can be seen on their way in all directions and it is not long before one has found something here, another there, that might be suitable, though often many miles distant. Successful scouts *dance* on their return, on the surface of the cluster; they indicate the distance and direction of the accommodation they have discovered, in the same way as the foragers show the way to a source of food. In consequence, ever-increasing numbers of dancers can be seen on the swarm; some point in one direction, others in another, some indicate places near by, others a considerable distance away, according to the various sites discovered. At the same time it can be seen that there is more excitement over some places than others. Just as the dances become exceedingly lively in the case of a rich harvest and become fainter and fainter with decreasing abundance of the nectar, so the scouts too dance with an intensity in proportion to the suitability of the discovery. This depends on: the size of the hole, on the sheltered position of the entrance (there must be no draughts in the dwelling place), on the smell (which must please the bees)—and on who knows how many other things besides!

Then within a few hours, or sometimes only during the course of several days, something really extraordinary happens. The most vivacious of the dancers who have found a selected place gain more and more followers; these have taken a good look at it and show their approval by making propaganda for it by dancing themselves. Also other dancers, who until now have canvassed for a less attractive dwelling place, become converted by the swirl of the successful ones. They follow their advice and look at this other accommodation until they too are convinced of its worth. Many of the bees which cannot show such enthusiasm as the lucky discoverers for *their* accommodation simply cease dancing altogether if things take this turn. Thus an agreement is reached; all dance the same measure and in the same direction. When everything is ready, the swarm dissolves, to fly off under the direction of hundreds of its members who already know the way to the objective which has been chosen as the best available.

There is much that man could learn from the bees, but he does not have the patience. Before the foregoing events have been brought to a conclusion, he interferes and draws the swarm into his hive—just as he so often destroys natural processes with his coarse hands for his own ends.

Bees dancing in the service of agri- as well as of apiculture

A traveller visiting a foreign country will do better if he speaks its language. The same applies to a bee-keeper in his dealings with his bees: if only he knows their "language" he will have a better chance of persuading them to follow his own intentions.

With summer, the time of exuberant flowering has passed. It is true that many plants are still in bloom, but the nectar-flow is no longer as abundant as it was earlier in the year. An experienced bee-keeper is aware of the fact that field thistles, for example, which now appear in their hundreds of thousands, with their millions of inflorescences, each surrounded by its green phyllaries, bidding fair to reach the sky, could still yield many a pound of honey. But the bees in his colonies have lost their former zest for foraging. The insects which we see most often busying themselves among those thistles are the bumble bees. Gifted with longer tongues, they are in a better position than the honey-bees to penetrate to the bottom of the corolla tubes of these plants. As for the bees, the nectar in these tubes is not sufficiently accessible to them to justify the summoning of reinforcements. The bee-keeper, looking at this state of affairs with concern, may wonder how he could persuade his bees to try and exploit those still profitable thistles instead of spending their time idling about in the hive.

If he tries to talk to the bees in their own language, he *can* actually suggest it to them. All he has to do, after having with the help of some honey and sugar-water enticed a few bees to approach a bunch of thistles, is to go on feeding them with a little sugar-water sprinkled on to the thistle blossoms. The bees who forage there will dance in the hive and show, by means of the flower scent they bring home, where their crop comes from and where to look for it. Their companions, aroused by their dances, will, in their turn, fly out in search of the thistle-scent that promises such a rich crop to them. In this way a bee-keeper may be able to increase considerably the number of his bees collecting nectar from the wild thistle.

For the actual practice of bee-keeping this method has been modified and at the same time simplified in various ways. Bee-keepers may be equally successful if, instead of making them feed on the thistles in the field, they offer to their bees a sugar solution pervaded by thistle scent, inside their own hive. They can easily obtain such a solution by soaking the blossoms in sugar-water for several hours. This holds good for thistle blossoms or for any other flowers for that matter, except those whose scent might be affected by this procedure, so that they would no longer be of any use. Flowers of the latter type are best offered in a small feeding-box placed in front of the entrance hole, with just a little sugar-water sprinkled on them. Using this and similar methods, progressive bee-keepers have, with very little effort on their part, obtained considerable yields of honey from wild thistles and other nectar-producing plants at a time when all their neighbours had long ceased to reap any harvest at all.

It is not only the bee-keeper who wants to direct the attention of the honey-bees to a particular crop. The farmer would often like to do the same in order to increase the chances of pollination, and so of seed production, in some of his plants. Seed production, the first condition for its cultivation as a crop is, for example, a difficult and uncertain matter in the case of one of our most important fodder crops, the red clover. Its flowers are normally frequented by humble-bees, as their nectar is not easily accessible to the honey-bee's tongue, which is not long enough to reach the bottom of the corolla tubes. Wherever red clover is grown as a crop, the number of humble-bees that happen to be about in the same area could not possibly suffice to cope with the pollination of its millions and millions of florets. Honey-bees, on the other hand, are not inclined to forage in a place which, for them, yields such a scanty crop as does a field of red clover, at least while there are more promising crops elsewhere. Consequently, the desired quantity of seed is produced only in those exceptional years in which the red clover happens to secrete nectar so abundantly that it tempts even the honey-bees to pay it regular visits. This grievance can be redressed, however. All we have to do is to place some beehives very close to the red clover fields. If we then condition the bees to its scent in the way we have just described, the number of their visits will increase to such an extent that, on the average, seed production may be raised by as much as forty per cent; in other words it can be relied upon to be sufficient for our needs.

Though this method of "control by scent" has not yet been widely used, experienced seedsmen, impressed by its success have quickly taken to it, and its application is likely to spread, particularly in those districts where poverty necessitates intensive exploitation of every inch of soil. The honey-pots of the bee-keeper can be filled, and the harvest of the farmer improved, if each of them is willing to make the small effort of telling the bees in their own "language" exactly where to work for him.

CHAPTER TWELVE

The Bee's Sense of Time

WE all know from our own experience what is meant by "sense of time". Though the degree of its reliability may vary from person to person, nobody will ever be found to be completely without it.

To give one example. Supposing we went on an excursion with a group of people none of whom had brought watches. If asked the time at the approach of noon, a few of them would guess that it was half-past eleven, or half-past twelve for that matter, while others might plump for times as different as 11 a.m. or 2 p.m. However, nobody would go as far as to suggest such extremes as, say, 8 a.m. or 7 p.m. They would be saved from such error, if by nothing else, by the state of their appetites or by a glance at the sun's position. To give an altogether different example—at this very moment I realize that I have spent some considerable time brooding over this sentence before setting it down, namely approximately two minutes, or at any rate more than thirty seconds, but less than ten minutes. This estimate of mine—which has obviously nothing to do with my being hungry, or my taking any clues from the sun's position—must be due to an awareness of the passage of time on my part, about the functioning of which we know very little, except that it is probably based on a variety of external and internal processes.

Animals, too, may show some appreciation of time. On the alpine pastures in the county of Salzburg, for example, one may see the cattle, accustomed to being stalled at eleven, gathering in front of the alpine herdsman's cottage shortly

137

before that time without any outside prompting. Everybody who has had dealings with animals will recall some experience of a similar kind, probably concerning domestic animals like dogs, cats, and horses, or perhaps some other mammals. All these animals are structurally much more similar to us than we are to insects.

The question whether an insect possesses any faculty at all comparable with our own appreciation of time is one of particular interest to the student of the honey-bee, and one which, as we shall see later, cannot be decided offhand. In the absence of an *a priori* answer, some relevant experiments must be carried out.

Again we start an artificial feeding-place by attracting bees to a table placed in the open, where they are fed from a sugar-water dish. Again the insects frequenting this place are marked so that we can recognize them individually. Instead of feeding the bees continuously, however, we proceed to feed them only at a particular time of the day, say between 4 and 6 p.m., outside of which period the dish is left empty. This is repeated daily. Such members of our group of marked bees as arrive to explore the feeding-place outside their appointed feeding-time, return to their hive without having achieved anything. On the other hand, all those who arrive between 4 and 6 p.m. will find the dish full of sugar-water and will therefore arouse the rest of their group by their dances. Soon these too will reappear at the feeding-place to busy themselves taking back a fresh supply of syrup.

For several days on end we continue, whenever the weather is fine, to feed the bees from 4 to 6 p.m. Then we carry out the final test. This time the same dish—empty—is put out for them all day long, while an observer sitting close by performs the tedious task of recording the behaviour of every single bee that happens to alight on the empty dish between the hours of 6 in the morning and 8 at night. During a first long period from 6 a.m. to 3.30 p.m., out of a group of six bees which had frequented the dish in the preceding days only one (marked as No. 11) arrives and explores the feeding place;

she makes her first appearance between 7 and 7.30 a.m., to return a second time soon after. Apart from this, it is completely deserted until the usual feeding time approaches: at 3.30 we notice quite a stir beginning and between 4 and 6 p.m. five of the six marked bees appear, between them paying a total of thirty-eight visits to the empty dish. In spite of their lack of success they keep returning to the dish at frequent intervals, some of them alighting on it as often as ten times in half an hour, examining it with great persistence, as if they were convinced that something must be found there at this time of the day. It is not until the end of their usual feeding period, towards 6 p.m., that the traffic begins to show signs of subsiding; soon the whole place lies deserted again. Our experiment has succeeded beyond all expectation. In the graph shown in fig. 50 we can see the number of the bees'

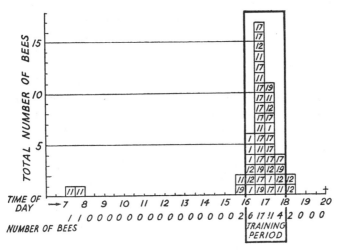

Fig. 50.   Result of an experiment on time sense. A few numbered bees had received sugar-water at an artificial feeding-place from 4 to 6 p.m. daily. On the day of the test (July 20, 1927) the feeding-dish remained empty all day, even during the training time. The hours are indicated along the horizontal axis. Above each half-hour, the number of bees that flew to the dish during this period is shown. Each square indicates a bee with its distinguishing number. Squares standing on top of one another with the same number mean that the same bee came to investigate several times from the hive to the dish within this half-hour (after Ingeborg Beling).

visits per time-unit plotted against the whole length of the observation time subdivided into half-hourly periods by short vertical lines. For reasons of emphasis the space for the training period from 4 to 6 p.m. has been enclosed in a black frame. Each bee visiting the empty dish is shown as a small square marked off with her number of identity. This graph gives a better idea of the measure of our success than any verbal description.

Similar experiments have been carried out with several different groups of bees, each group being trained to find its food at a different time of the day. In each case the outcome of the experiment has proved beyond any doubt that after only a few days of training the bees had learned to appear, with quite surprising punctuality, at any period of the day during which they had become used to being fed.

The success of our first experiments tempted us to put the bee's memory for time to an even severer test: a group of marked bees was fed daily during two separate periods extending from 5.45 to 9.45 a.m. and from 6.30 p.m. to nightfall, respectively. After a whole week of this training, the final test was performed, again with an observer sitting close by and recording the number of individual visits to an empty feeding-dish for every half-hour of the day. The result was a brilliant success. Fourteen marked bees out of an original total of fifteen appeared regularly at the feeding-place, thus clearly indicating that they had been trained with complete success to come for their food during two separate periods of the day.

It has proved possible to train bees to arrive at their feeding place during three, four, or even five separate periods in the course of a single day. In fig. 51, the result of a three-period training is shown. We can see that the tendency of the bees to arrive a little before their appointed time, which had been already noticeable in the single-period training experiments, has become much more obvious. No one could call such behaviour inappropriate. The world is so full of hungry creatures, all intent on snatching the best morsels from each other's mouths, that we should not blame the bees for trying to be on the spot too early rather than too late. If we ignore this slight deviation, we must admit that the graph shown in fig. 51 makes it plain for all to see that their six days' training to three different periods of the day has not been wasted on

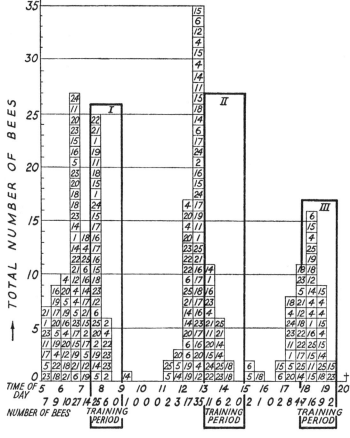

Fig. 51. *Result of an experiment with training at three different times. Training period six days. On the day of the test (August 13, 1928) all of the nineteen numbered bees came to the feeding-place, at the times indicated above, although there was no food to be had all day. See also the more detailed description in fig. 50 (after Ingeborg Beling).*

our bees, especially as there was not a drop of sugar-water to be had at their usual feeding place during the whole of August 13th—the date of their final test.

Findings like these prompt us to ask ourselves, where, then, does the bee carry her watch? Is it perhaps in her stomach, causing her to leave the hive and rush towards the feeding-place when it begins to stir at the approach of her appointed feeding time? This explanation is not likely to be correct if only for the following reason: a bee does not come to the feed-ing-dish in order to drink her fill, like other insects do; she calls there to collect the food for the colony, to be stored inside the hive. If she wants to satisfy her own hunger she has no need to fly out at all, but can easily extend her tongue towards one of these honey stores while remaining seated on the combs, where she spends most of her free time anyhow. Her foraging time is therefore not a "feeding time" in the true meaning of the word.

What finally exploded the above-mentioned explanation was the outcome of the following test. For several days we offered our bees a permanent source of sugar-water which was increased or made more concentrated during certain hours than during the rest of the day. In this way, their stomachs did not remain empty for any length of time and they con-tinued to forage. Yet on the day of the final test they arrived at the empty dish at the observer's table with distinctly increased zest during their habitual period of "abundant feeding". Could it be that, like the wayfarer wanting to know the time, the bee had taken her clue from the sun's position? This would appear a fairly plausible explanation for an insect like the honey-bee which has in certain conditions been shown to pay such great attention to the direction of the rays of the sun. But whether this factor is also involved in her remember-ing the time of the day cannot be solved by guessing. It can only be revealed to us if again we perform the appropriate experiment.

It is possible to transfer a whole colony of bees to a room that can be completely blacked out. Here they may thrive for weeks or even for months on end in spite of the fact that their range of flight is limited by four solid walls. It is true that none of the bees would venture out of the hive while the place is kept dark. However if we now keep our room permanently illuminated with a powerful electric light—thus eliminating all periodic change of light and dark—it should be impossible for the bee to draw any conclusion about the time of day by looking at the sun or estimating the brightness of the light. However, even these bees, in their enclosed space, may be attracted to a feeding spot in the usual way and trained to look there for food at certain periods of the day, as successfully as are bees trained in the open—rather more successfully, inasmuch as in the artificial conditions of constant illumination we can extend the hours of training as far into the night as we like without experiencing any change in the bee's response.

It is now clear that we are dealing here with beings who, seemingly without needing a clock, possess a memory for time, dependent neither on a feeling of hunger nor an appreciation of the sun's position, and which, like our own appreciation of time, seems to defy any further analysis. So far as precision is concerned it is doubtful if we are a match for the bees, as we can only estimate correctly the length of a fairly short interval, whereas the bee, even in the monotony of the illuminated room, is able to recognize the hour of the day at which it had been fed.

Though bees can easily be trained to a twenty-four-hour cycle, they seem to be unable to grasp any other kind of rhythm. For example, if we feed them every nineteen hours in our artificially-lighted room, they will give no sign of having learned to understand that interval even after several weeks of training. Neither do they learn to respond to a forty-eight-hour rhythm. Bees that were used to finding their food every forty-eight hours, when tested for two days and nights after several weeks of this training, appeared at the feeding place exactly twenty-four hours after their latest meal. This gives us the impression that what is being remembered by the bee

is not so much the length of the interval between two successive feeding periods as the precise hour of the day at which she
has become accustomed to find her food.

We have to consider one of two possibilities. Either bees
are influenced by a daily periodicity which we ourselves cannot perceive, and of the existence of which we are not even
aware, or they carry their own clock along with them, in the
form of the metabolic processes going on in their bodies. If
the second hypothesis is correct, then our failure to train
them to a nineteen-hour rhythm as well as to a forty-eight-
hour rhythm means that they are so firmly bound up with
their normal habits to a twenty-four-hour cycle, that they
simply cannot be induced to remember any other interval.

The following experiment could determine finally which of
the two theories is true. A colony of bees, trained say, in
Hamburg, to look for food at a certain hour of the day, is
tested in an ocean liner bound on a westward voyage. While

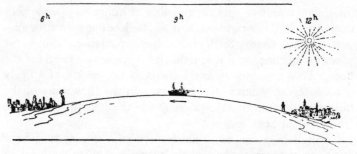

Fig. 52. An imaginary test across the Atlantic.

it is noon in Hamburg it would still be 9 a.m. in some spot in
the middle of the Atlantic, and only 6 a.m. in New York.
Supposing they responded to the precise hour of the day to
which they had been trained, then the bees will arrive at their
feeding place whenever their appointed hour strikes at the
particular point the liner had happened to reach on her
voyage. If, on the other hand, their response depends upon
the rate of their metabolic processes, then all the way across

they should arrive at their feeding-dish according to Hamburg time. This experiment still remains to be carried out.

The possession of this highly-developed sense of time might appear to be of no special significance in the life of the bee, particularly as the meal times we devise for her are of our own fixing and have apparently nothing to do with any rhythm in nature. However, some such connection does exist, as nature, like ourselves, provides meals for the bees only at definite times. A similar rule holds for the secretion of nectar. Most flowers, while offering a good nectar crop for a few hours, produce little or nothing during the rest of the day. The time of maximal production which may fall into morning, noon, or afternoon, as the case may be, remains constant for each species of plant. If we remember that bees show a high degree of "flower constancy"—that is to say that an individual bee will keep returning to one particular kind of flower over a period of several days—we can see at once that the existence of a period of maximal output in the flower on which they are foraging is bound to keep a group of bees very busy for part of the day while leaving them idle for the rest of it. And the best place for an idle bee is inside the hive, where she is safe from the dangerous outside world.

And in fact staying at home is what the members of any foraging group will do during a temporary drying-up of their particular food source—always with the exception of a few scouts who will fly out from time to time in order to explore the situation. As soon as such a scout bee notices that her flower is producing its crop once more she dances on the combs exactly as she did after her first discovery of it (see pp. 100 ff), thus summoning anew the rest of her own group. In the case of a crop drying up at irregular intervals, some scouts have to be on the wing all the time so as not to miss the moment when it becomes worth exploiting again. Conversely, if a crop is available only during one limited period of the day, then the scouts will soon learn to give up exploring the place during the intervals when there is no chance of finding food there.

The next question is, whether a group of bees is more strongly affected by a careful training to a time of day, or by the stimulation of dancers. In order to decide this we trained a group of marked bees to come for their food every day between 5.30 a.m. and 10 a.m. The training completed, we offered a new crop just after the feeding-period had ended, when a few of our marked foragers were still hanging about the place. As was to be expected, these few went on foraging even after 10 a.m., and that they must have continued to dance in the hive as well may be concluded from the appearance of new unmarked bees at the feeding-dish. Yet not one of their companions which had only recently shared their foraging returned to the feeding-place as a result of their dancing. It almost looked as if they could not believe dancers who tried to summon them after their accustomed foraging time. One glance at our observation hive was enough to show us that this assumption was wrong and that the correct explanation was this: all the dances are performed within a limited space not far from the entrance hole. Now the bees trained to forage at a certain period of the day will at the end of this period withdraw to a quiet spot near the edge of a comb, or to a remote corner of the hive, where they can escape the hurly-burly of the "ballroom". There are even bees who may be relied upon to be found sitting in their favourite spots whenever they are not foraging. This whole group of drowsy insects will suddenly come to life again at the approach of the meal time: crawling up from every direction, they will now hasten towards the particular part of the combs where they are likely to meet the first of the returning scout bees. What had happened in our last experiment, where the period of feeding had been extended beyond its usual limit, was that most of the members of our foraging group had by then retired to their familiar sitting-out places where the dancers could not possibly get at them. Hence we had waited in vain for their reappearance. They cannot adjust themselves to what seems to them an interference with the natural course of events, contrary to all the familiar rules.

The bees' sense of time is of the greatest importance and affects also their orientation in space; for the sun is only of use as a compass if one can tell the time of day.

So, often, when our watch has come to grief, we should envy the bees who carry an unbreakable watch in their bodies.

CHAPTER THIRTEEN

The Bee's Mental Capacity

THIS chapter will be short. So little is known about the mental capacity of the honey-bee that it is better not to say too much about it.

One point, however, should be stressed. The reader who has learnt with what ingenuity our bees construct their hexagonal cells; how they can be trained to come for their food; by what skilful methods they collect the nectar and pollen for their colony; and finally how energetically they dispose of their drones when they are no longer of any use to the community, may feel inclined to credit the honey-bee with a fair degree of intelligence. However, the fact that an action is expedient is in itself no proof that it has been carried out with any degree of consciousness.

We speak of an intelligent action when someone responds in an appropriate way to a situation that is completely new to him, making use, in the process, of some earlier experience. The prerequisites for such an action are: first, a good memory for events of the past, secondly a grasp of the situation in hand, and finally the ability of mentally associating them.

Bees most certainly possess the first of these attributes, a retentive memory. In the course of the numerous experiments described in earlier chapters we have had plenty of chances of making sure of this. When trained to look for a certain colour, bees will return to it even though they had been prevented from leaving the hive by several days of rainy weather. On the other hand, if in a training experiment a scent is presented to them though only for a very short time it will be remembered for many weeks, perhaps for the rest of their lives.

Nor can there be any doubt as to the bee's capacity for forming some mental associations. The very fact that bees who had been offered food inside a blue box had thereby successfully been trained to fly towards the blue colour in search of their food is sufficient proof of their having "grasped" the connection between the blue colour they had perceived on entering the box, and the food they had found inside it.

All the same, because of its extraordinarily narrow range, we cannot form a very high opinion of the bee's mental capacity.

A relevant story comes to my mind. The mason-bee, though it is a near relative of the honey-bee, leads a solitary life. For each separate egg, this bee builds a globular clay cell into which she puts exactly enough honey to feed the larva from its emergence from the egg to the time of its pupation. After accumulating these food stores she lays her egg on top of them. She then closes the entrance to the cell, thus protecting her offspring against any interference from outside. This done, she proceeds to build another cell, without bothering any more about her first child's fate.

The following experiment has been reported by an observer of the mason-bee. While one of the mother bees was busying herself collecting food from flowers for a cell of hers which had just been completed except for the lid, he broke open the floor of this cell, producing a yawning hole which the bee on her return examined with her feelers. Obviously she must have been aware of the hole, yet it did not occur to her to fill it, though she could have done so quite easily. Instead, she proceeded to dispose of her load in the usual way, with the result that all the nectar fell through the gap; and as this performance was repeated whenever the bee returned from one of her foraging flights, load after load was wasted. Her failure to fill the cell being obvious, we would have expected her to take one of two possible courses of action. Either she would continue indefinitely bringing in food with unremitting zeal, or else realize the futility of her action and abandon the cell. However, in fact she followed neither of these courses. Instead, she went on foraging until she had collected exactly enough food to feed a larva under normal conditions; this done she laid an egg, which of course fell through the bottom of the cell like everything else, and finally she carefully topped the cell with a lid while the big hole at its lower end was still gaping.

As I have not seen this experiment personally, I cannot vouch for this description being correct in every detail. At any rate, even if it did not happen exactly in this way, the story has been put together with great ingenuity, so closely does it fit with our previous experience of other insects, including the honey-bee itself. There is, to my knowledge, not one example on record of a really intelligent action having been performed by a honey-bee. Even in our training experiments the bees failed to respond whenever the task set them differed slightly from those they had been accustomed to perform in the course of their flower visits which must have been carried out throughout a period of hundreds of thousands of years. The ability to grasp the connection, for example, between a flower's nectar or pollen and its scent is bound to be part and parcel of the bee's inborn mental equipment. However, as soon as we replace the flower scent with bad smells we jeopardize the success of their training, though the fact that the bees enter the box containing this smell without showing the slightest hesitation should prove that in itself it is not repellent to them. In other special experiments, we have been able to prove that the bee's perception of a bad smell is just as acute as her perception of a flower scent. But in all their long history the ancestors of our experimental bees have never found nectar occurring in connection with a bad smell, and apparently it is impossible for any individual bee to form a mental association between the two.

We have seen that our bees' learning ability is restricted to those factors which, in their normal surroundings, have a meaning for them, and to which they have been accustomed since prehistoric times. Our modern bee remembers the blue colour, or the scent of rose blossom, near which she had discovered her food, just like untold generations of bees before her. From them has been handed down to her, as her mental heritage, the ability to build hexagonal cells, to fill her pollen baskets, to advertise a worthwhile crop by means of dances, and to kill off the drones in her hive at the appropriate time. According to strict laws, long-prevailing conditions have produced traditional habitual reactions.

Nobody can state with certainty whether the bees are conscious of any of their own actions. Nor has any human being yet unravelled the mystery of how and when their ancestors, for the first time, acquired those abilities, which in their present perfected form are being handed down, as its common heritage, to each new generation in turn.

CHAPTER FOURTEEN

Enemies and Diseases of Bees

P ROSPERITY has its dangers: it may arouse the envy of the have-nots. Not a single colony would have survived if bees had not poisoned weapons to defend their sweet winter stores. In the virgin forest of bygone times, the original home of the honey-bee, it was mainly the sweet-toothed bear who stripped many a colony of its honey stores. As bears became scarce, man himself followed suit, with even greater success. We must remember that sugar was once a rare and expensive substance. Even today we may occasionally admire, in someone's house, an antique silver sugar-box which has a lock, though its key may long since have been lost, reminding us of the great value that was set on its contents by our great-grandfathers. Naturally at that time honey was very much more sought after as a sweetening agent than it is now, while a few centuries earlier there was no other sugar available in Europe than the nectar collected from flowers by the honey-bee. Small wonder, then, that it was man himself who became the bee's worst enemy. Only in recent times relations between man and bee have changed for the better. Nowadays man, having become attached to his bees in the course of time, bestows his loving care on them in exchange only for that amount of honey that exceeds their own needs. Gone, too, are the romantic days when our forests were populated by bears. As for the smaller fry hankering for honey—the ants, wasps, death's-head moth, and the like, or an occasional mouse or two—these may at times become very tiresome but they will hardly ever do any serious harm to a colony.

Yet it would be wrong to assume that bees enjoy an undisturbed peace today.   One can still fill whole books with
descriptions of their enemies.   In fact there is a wide choice
of such books.   But in the present one we shall mention only
those which are of particular importance, and, at the same
time, have rather fascinating qualities.

There is, for instance, one insect belonging to the tribe of
digger-wasps (*Philanthus*), which in German is called a
"Bienenwolf" or "bee-wolf" because of its voracious appetite
for bees.   Though related to colony-forming wasps, about
which more presently, all members of the digger-wasp family
lead a solitary life.   They hunt all kinds of insects to provide
food for their grubs.   Each separate species pursues its own
particular type of prey, tracking it down and overpowering it
with consummate skill.   The Philanthus wasp has selected
as her prey the heavily-armed honey-bee.   Much more agile
though not very much taller than her victim, she pounces
down on it when it is about to visit a flower, inserts her sting
into her victim's throat, or alternately into the soft joint
between the prothorax and the mesothorax, as if she knew
exactly the bee's most vulnerable spot (see fig. 53).   This
done, she clasps that part of the bee's abdomen which

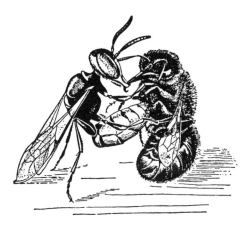

Fig. 53.   A digger wasp paralyses a bee with its sting.

contains the honey-bag, squeezes out the nectar it contains through its mouth, and consumes it. Then carrying the bee along with her, holding it tightly underneath her abdomen, the digger-wasp takes it to a hole in the sandy soil from where a sloping shaft leads into a brood chamber prepared earlier for this purpose. Having spread out from three to four slaughtered bees on the floor of this place, the wasp deposits one single egg on the body of one of the bees. She may then either continue her activities in another brood chamber of the same nest or she may start digging a new hole. As soon as the larva, which resembles the maggot of a fly, has hatched from its egg, it starts devouring, one by one, all the bees that had been put so conveniently at its disposal (pl. xxiva). As they have only been paralysed, but not killed by the sting of the wasp, they remain as fresh as any cold storage meat, helplessly abandoned to the attack of the inert maggot which, after growing to its full size, pupates inside the brooding chamber, to emerge from it in the following summer when, as a young wasp, it in turn adopts its mother's vicious craft.

There are areas where the digger-wasps find such favourable conditions for their nest building that they may do a lot of damage. For example, there is a place in the potash region of Thuringia and Hesse in Germany, in the vale of the river Werra, where refuse dumps of brown coal ash and of sediments of salt have accumulated which suited the wasps so well that their numbers came to present a serious threat to apiculture, and many farmers had to give up bee-keeping until the pest had been successfully eradicated by expensive government measures. A careful survey revealed that in burrows made within an area of 150 by 100 yards nearly two million bees had fallen victim to the wasps in a single year, that is to say the equivalent of the entire population of about fifty colonies of bees.

If the digger-wasp is like one of those heavily armed robber barons of the Middle Ages, the bee-louse on the other hand is of a very different disposition. Far from being a louse, as its name would suggest, it belongs to the tribe of flies, being one

of those peculiar species that have lost their wings as a consequence of their parasitic way of life. Bee-lice owe their name
mainly to their habit of roaming about among the piles of fur
that cover the bee's body, much in the manner of real lice.
In this activity they are assisted by claws at the tips of their
feet, which enable them to cling to hair with safety. Their
place of preference is the fur of the queen, from whose body
we may pick up dozens of these creatures, while somewhat
smaller numbers can be found on worker-bees in any colony
infested with these pests. When the louse feels like feeding, it
moves on to the head of its host, tapping her lip with its legs
while holding on to her mouth (pl. xxivb). This is the spot
where her companions tickle her when telling her they are
hungry in their "feeler language". The bee thus addressed is
easily taken in by the little imposter perched up on her head,
and obliges by opening her mouth and letting a droplet of
honey exude from it. Living on the queen, who receives her
regular meals from the mouths of the worker-bees acting as
her nurses, the "royal lice" may simply take their share without even having to beg for it. Such behaviour seems harmless enough. Yet a heavily infested queen may get upset by
the lice and, in consequence, not lay as many eggs as she ought
to. The watchful bee-keeper will pick out the queen and rid
her of her unwanted guests by blowing smoke at her while
holding her in the hollow of his hand.

An insect that may be coupled with the predatory wasp and
the pilfering fly as a particularly noxious enemy of the honey-
bee is the wax-moth, a moth related to the well-known
clothes'-moth with which it has much in common. Both are
small moths developing in the normal way. The caterpillar
emerges from the egg, feeds all the time until it has fattened
considerably, then is transformed into the pupa. After a
period of rest, the cocoon bursts open to release the adult
moth or "imago". Neither of the two moths is able to do any
harm at that stage, because their abortive mouth parts do not
function at all, and during the short weeks of their adult life
they have to subsist on fat they have accumulated in their

bodies as caterpillars. In both cases it is the caterpillar that does all the damage. The woollen threads and such like that are attacked by the clothes'-moth larva, and the wax of which combs are built, which is greedily devoured by the larva of the wax-moth, are for them high-grade foodstuffs, but they cannot be dealt with by the digestive juices of ordinary living beings. It is the particular secret of these larvae that their highly-specialized digestive juices are able to split up just those food sources. The horny substance of which for example hair consists, is a protein that contains all the necessary elements for building up an animal's body. Wax on the other hand, a substance related to fat, is free of protein. Accordingly, wax-moths will not thrive on pure bees-wax alone, but depend on getting supplementary food that contains protein. Of this they are bound to find an ample supply inside the combs, in the form of pollen and other residues, as well as waste products left over from the secretions of the rightful owners of the hive.

A comb invaded by wax-moths presents a sorry sight indeed. It is furrowed by the food galleries made by the caterpillars, as well as sullied by their excrements and by the webs which they spin to protect their burrows. Each caterpillar lives in a silken tunnel of its own spinning, again like the larvae of the clothes'-moth. As long as a bee colony is healthy and strong, wax-moths can do little damage. But a weak colony may lose the ability to cope with these invaders. It is in the stores of unused combs, neglected by the careless bee-keeper, that wax-moths do their greatest damage, destroying everything completely, as no bees are present to prevent them.

So far we have dealt with robbers and parasites only. If the parasites are small enough to get inside a bee's body they may actually cause a disease. It was in the beginning of this century that an infectious bee disease, which first occurred in the Isle of Wight, and later throughout England, spread from there all over the rest of Europe, ravaging the bee colonies everywhere. Bees infested with this disease can easily be distinguished by their sluggish flight. Unable to remain on the

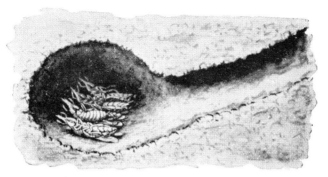

XXIV (a) Nest of the digger wasp. The larva making a meal off a paralysed bee (after a drawing by H. Thiem)

(b) Worker bee with two bee-lice, one waiting for food at the bee's mouth

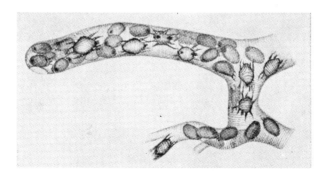

(c) Breathing tube in the chest of a bee infested with mites. Between the mites can be seen their eggs, which are nearly as big as the mother mites (after Morgenthaler, much enlarged)

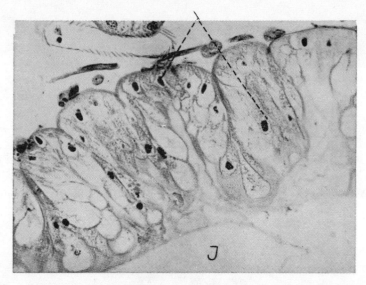

XXV (a) *Section through the intestinal wall of a healthy bee.* N, *nuclei of the cells of the intestinal wall;* J, *inside space of the intestinal tube*

(b) *Section through the intestinal wall of a bee sick with* Nosema. *The intestinal cells are filled with countless spores. They have been darkened in colour to show up. Some of them (at* X) *have already penetrated the inner space of the intestine. In this way the spores reach the excreta and help to spread the infection (much enlarged. Prepared by G. Reng; photo by A. Langwald)*

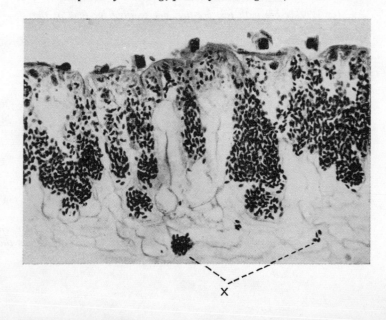

wing they come gliding down to perish below in no time. Whole groups of colonies may thus die out in a case of heavy infestation. It was not until 1920 that the cause of the disease was discovered. This was found to be a very small mite entering through the spiracles of the thorax into the trachea, where it reproduces freely. Mites are small spiders, and most of their many species show undesirable traits, some spoiling stores of flour, some living in cheese, while others again cause scabies in the skin of dirty people. One species of these mites have bestowed their attention on the honey-bee. Inside its tracheal tubes they find a domicile conveniently protected from all outside interference. In order to suck the nutritious bee blood, they have only to thrust their beaks through the walls of these tubes. If they reproduce on a grand scale their bodies and large eggs, together with the remains of their blood meals and excrements, will finally block the bee's breathing passages (pl. xxivc). Noxious substances excreted by them may further contribute to the death of their host. A slight infestation, though harmless in itself, may be all the more dangerous as, going unnoticed for a long time, it may remain a source of infection for other bee colonies.

While this disease affects the breathing tubes there are other diseases attacking the bees' digestive system. One of the most pernicious diseases of this type is the *Nosema* disease which takes its name from the parasite, *Nosema apis*, that causes it. This belongs to a group of creatures with which we have no conscious dealings in our daily life because they are so very much smaller even than a mite. The *Nosema* parasite is one of the so-called uni-cellular creatures which can be seen only with the help of a good microscope. It shows certain similarities to the well-known *amœba*, which may be described as a little lump of mucus come alive that crawls about with sluggish movements in the mud of water puddles. The group of so-called *sporozoa* to which the *Nosema* parasite belongs has developed along rather different lines. They have chosen to lead the life of a parasite, taking up their domicile inside the cells and organs of other animals, living at their expense, and

doing them great damage by their presence. If they reproduce
at a high enough rate they may even kill their hosts, thus
destroying the very basis of their existence. However, nature
has seen to it that the tribe of these little fiends does not suddenly die out. While still surrounded by an abundance of
food, they form internal cysts that enclose their young between solid walls, thus resembling the spores of plants.
Hence the name of *sporozoa* or *spore animalcules* (pl. xxva
and b). These spores are extremely resistant to all kinds of
adverse influences, able to survive not only their parent germs
but also their hosts, by several months or even several years,
during which time they go on spreading the epidemic disease.
Parasites gradually destroy the cells lining the bee's chyle-
stomach which they had invaded. In an advanced stage of
this disease the intestine itself is filled with innumerable spores
which, being expelled with the bee's fæces, become a danger
to the remaining, still healthy bees. It is true that this disease
in its widely spread form may often take a comparatively mild
course. However, outbreaks not infrequently occur that are
severe enough to cause the bee-keeper serious worry.

"Children's diseases" are also known to attack the bee
tribe. In completing this little survey with one of them, we
come across a type of beings as cause of diseases which approach even more closely the limit of visibility. The germs
that cause most of our epidemic diseases belong to very small
plant-like beings called bacteria. Typhoid, cholera, diphtheria,
tuberculosis, and many other plagues are caused by these
inconspicuous parasites which are just visible under a high-
power microscope. According to individual taste, they settle
in some organ of the body where they may cause local symptoms apart from the more general symptoms of a serious
nature that usually accompany these. In spite of measuring
only a few thousandths of a millimetre they achieve this
through their enormous rate of reproduction and their excretion of noxious substances. Yet in the history of human
diseases we know of no case where the attack is so sudden and
overpowering, leading to wholesale and speedy destruction of

the body as it is in the malignant *foul brood* disease of the bees.
This attacks only the brood, that is to say larvae still growing
inside their brood cells.   Scientists have found that it is caused
by a certain form of bacteria that multiply at such a rate
inside the larvae, particularly when they are about to pupate,
as to pervade and finally destroy their whole body.   The
infested larvae change colour and gradually turn into a slimy
mass that can be pulled out into threads.   The very care
bestowed on the brood by the worker-bee now becomes a
threat to the remaining healthy brood: while purging the cells
of the remains of disintegrating bodies, in preparation for new
eggs, the workers become themselves contaminated with the
germs of the bacteria, which they then transfer to the new
healthy larvae to whom they next act as brood nurses.

Enough of these horrid creatures that spell disease and
doom to the bees.   Let us now return to healthy and cheerful
topics, casting a glance in quite another direction on the way.

CHAPTER FIFTEEN

Other Insect Communities

EVERYBODY must some time or other have stood and watched an ant heap, which with all its hustle and bustle might have reminded him of a colony of honey-bees; and many will probably have seen a wasps' nest in the roof of a barn; but I expect that only a few have ever had an opportunity of ferreting out the nest of a bumble-bee, which not even the expert eye can easily find.

All three: bumble-bees, wasps, and ants, are closely related to the honey-bee, just as dogs, cats, lions, and many other "beasts of prey" are zoologically more or less related to each other. Just as there are plenty of mammals, apart from these, which are quite unrelated in appearance and structure, such as cattle, horses, hares, mice, so there are numerous species of insects quite unlike the bee in habit and structure: flies, beetles, butterflies, and so on. Among these we look in vain for the slightest signs of any tendency to form colonies. In each group related to the bee this tendency seems to be inherent. Admittedly there are also many members which lead a solitary life, but all insects that form colonies belong to this group, with the single exception of the termites, which are in a class by themselves. They are not found in this country, and are thus not discussed in this book.

The diversity of organization and colony formation that has developed among the members of the group of closely related insects to which the bees, bumble-bees, wasps, and ants belong, is quite amazing. It would be easy to devote a whole book to each separate group without ever boring the reader.

However, here we can only consider, and then very briefly, the ways in which these communities either differ from, or resemble that of the honey-bee.

The ant community

Of all the social insects mentioned so far, ants differ most strikingly from bees in the way their societies are formed. An ant-hill piled up artlessly from pine needles gathered together by the horse-ant has little in common with the ingenious waxen building constructed by a colony of bees. And those wingless inhabitants that can be seen crawling over their heap hastily, unsteadily, and aimlessly seem to bear little relation to their winged cousins the bees darting about so assuredly on their visits to the flowers. Yet in spite of great differences in habits and appearance, the colonies have fundamentally the same organization.

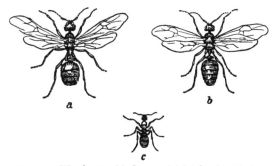

Fig. 54. *Wood ants.* (a) *Queen.* (b) *Male.* (c) *Worker.*

In every colony of ants, just as in every colony of bees, we find three different types (fig. 54): the queen, or fully developed female; the worker, or undeveloped female, whose fertility has been suppressed; and, at certain periods, the male. A bee colony has only one queen, but in an ant colony five, ten, or in very large colonies even as many as hundreds may be found living peaceably together. As with bees, the majority of ants are workers, several hundreds of thousands in a large community. The males are winged, and have brief lives. The queens, who may live for several years, have wings for a few days only, and the workers never. Ants may justly be called "children of the earth", and for that reason alone their way of life is inevitably different from that of bees, true "children of the air".

The ant's home is apparently a mound built of innumerable pine needles, pieces of stick, dry grass blades, and so on, collected by the workers (pl. xxvia). But it does not only live above ground; beneath the mound many passages and

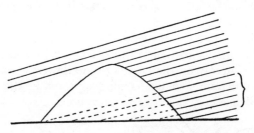

Fig. 55

chambers have been dug deep in the earth. Ants cannot, like bees, produce their own heat. The high temperature needed for the rearing of the brood has to be provided by the sun. Now, if the nest were flat the rays of the morning sun would strike it at an oblique angle and would not warm it up. But the domed shape of the ant-hill enables it to catch and utilize these rays, and this seems to be its main function (fig. 55). Even in the early hours of a sunny summer morning there may be quite a considerable rise of temperature in the upper layers, and the workers bring the eggs and grubs to them in order to keep them warm. They continue all day dragging them from chamber to chamber to catch the right conditions of warmth and humidity. Every evening they block up the entrances to keep out the cool night air and carry the brood down to the lower regions, where heat has accumulated during the day and will last longest. The doors are not opened until the next morning, when eggs, larvae, and pupae are again transported back to the surface if the weather is fine.

Unable to compensate for summer variations of temperature, ants are, of course, quite powerless against the cold of winter. In late autumn they withdraw to the lowermost part of their nest where they are well protected from frost. There they hibernate through the bad months and so have no need of winter stores. By the time they are awakened by the sun their food is ready for them in the open fields. It is not, however, the prospect of flowers that attracts them to the surface again. The ants' feeding habits are not so poetic as those of the bees. Their diet consists mainly of other insects which, though often larger, succumb to the poisonous mass attack of these nimble creatures, and are dragged, dead or alive, into the nest. A large colony may in one day collect a bag of some thousands of moths, caterpillars, and beetles. By destroying such pests they render an important service to the forest. These are their staple diet; but honey and sugar are their favourite food, as many housewives have found to their dismay. The normal source of supply is neither the housewife's jam-pot nor the blossoms of flowers whose deep corolla is usually inaccessible to the mouth of an ant, but the greenfly, which sucks the sap from juicy plant stems. These creatures live amid such an abundance of food that they excrete, unchanged, great quantities of this nutritious sugar. This sugar excretion, "honey-dew", is carefully collected by the ants and brought back to the nest; the providers of it are carefully cherished and protected from attack. Some ants even go so far as to carry their greenflies down to the depths of their nest in the autumn, where they hibernate and are brought up again in spring: like a farmer who takes his dairy cattle out of their winter stables for the spring grazing.

The queens do no foraging. They remain hidden in the nest completely taken up with egg-laying activities. The white grubs which hatch out are, like those of bees, without eyes, wings, or legs. Unlike the bee grub, born to inherit a single neat cell, they lie in piles inside their living chambers (pl. xxvib). Nevertheless they are carefully fed and nursed by the workers, who carry them to the warmest places, and hide them away safely in a remote part of the nest if danger threatens. When the larvae have grown to their full size they turn into chrysalises, first spinning an oval-shaped cocoon which encases the whole body. These cocoons containing a chrysalis are often sold as bird food under the name of "ants' eggs". Real ants' eggs are, of course, much smaller. By carefully pulling apart the threads of a cocoon we can discern the shape of the ant inside, complete but still pale in colour, ready to emerge from its case after a due period of rest.

One of the main differences between bees and ants lies in the way a new colony is started. Each summer winged males and females appear in the nest, sometimes—in large colonies —in vast numbers. If the weather is fine they climb up and out of the nest at a given hour and rise in the air like a column of smoke, never to return. This swarming movement of "flying ants", though it may recall the swarming of bees, is in fact entirely different. We remember that in the case of the swarming bees half of the workers of a colony may leave the hive in a swarm that forms round the old queen to found a new colony, while the remaining workers obtain a new queen. In the case of ants, however, the swarm consists only of young males and females who leave the nest on their nuptial flight. Once in the air they meet swarms from other colonies; the various males and females meet in the air, mate, and fall to the ground. The males, having performed the sole function of their life, soon die, while the fertilized females set about founding new colonies of their own. They are exposed to so many dangers and enemies, especially on their nuptial flight, that very few survive to fulfil their destiny.

The young fertilized queen starts by shedding her wings, which are no longer of any use and may be an actual hindrance in her new activity. No great effort is called for, as they are but loosely attached to her body. She spreads them out and rubs and presses them against the earth with the help of her legs, and they easily fall off. Next she excavates a little cave in the earth and blocks up the entrance from the inside. Here, all alone, she is to lay the first eggs from which she will

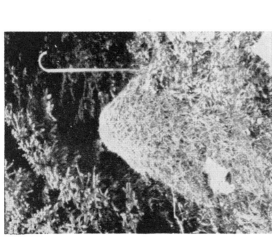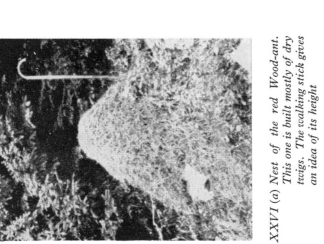

(b) Section of part of an ant heap. Passages and chambers with eggs above; larvae, chamber in middle; and pupae (so called 'ants-eggs'), bottom chamber (after André from Buytendijk)

XXVI (a) *Nest of the red Wood-ant. This one is built mostly of dry twigs. The walking stick gives an idea of its height*

XXVII (a) Wasps' nest attached to a rafter

(b) Wasps' nest with part of its outer covering removed. Inside, the combs are joined together by means of buttresses

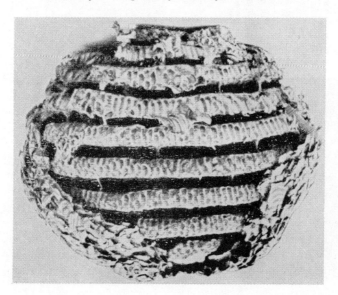

breed and rear the first worker-ants. Unable to go out and
bring food into her place of self-inflicted captivity, she has to
live on the fat she carries with her everywhere in her own body.
A principal source of supply are the strong flight muscles
inside her chest, which, now superfluous, gradually disintegrate, while their substance migrates into other parts of her
body, and into the eggs that are developing within her. The
young brood are fed in their turn on her saliva and with the
surplus eggs, which are given to a few selected larvae. She

*Fig. 56.   Queen Red Ant with brood, showing one much larger than the rest.
(Magnification × 3; after Dr. Eidmann).*

begins by choosing one (fig. 56) and nursing it till it is full
size, while the rest get only just enough to keep them alive.
Only when the first has fully grown and pupated does she
repeat the process with a second and then a third larva. It
seems that the queen does not wish to risk distributing her
limited food stocks too lavishly among all her offspring in
case there is not enough left for any one of them to complete
its development. As soon as these have pupated and emerged
from their pupa cases as the first of her new worker-ants, they
will pierce the wall of their prison in order to bring in new
building material for the common nest. From now on the
new colony begins to flourish.

   Having said all this, I must add that what I have described
is only one of the many ways in which a new ant colony is
founded, only one way of feeding, one sort of ant. There are

many different kinds of ant, many varieties of behaviour and appearance. Not all build ant-hills: many build nests under stones or inside old tree-trunks. Similarly we may find all kinds of peculiarities in ways of feeding and appearance. Even the workers of the same species may differ in form; and other ways of founding a new colony be seen. Many more striking features of ant life might be described here, but, after all, this is not meant to be a treatise on the life of the ant.

The colony of wasps

A wasps' nest, as shown in pl. xxviia, is constructed of soft, fragile, paper-like material of a grey or brown colour, and is usually to be found attached to a rafter or something similar by its upper end. Its lower end has an opening through which the wasps fly in and out. This balloon-like structure, made up of several layers, is only the outer cover comparable to the wooden hive enclosing a colony of bees. Inside this cover we find the actual nest (pl. xxviib) consisting of several combs made up of hexagonal cells. These are very much like the combs we see inside a beehive, except that they are arranged horizontally and have cells only on one side, made not of wax but of the same material as the outer cover, and with entrances pointing downward.

Wasps built their nests like this long before man had discovered how to make paper. In fact, the material used in building both the combs and the outer cover, being finely shredded wood bonded with some kind of cement, is not unlike paper. One may often see wasps settling on wooden fences, planks, or telegraph poles scraping off fine splinters with their powerful jaws. Having thus gathered building material they then cement it together with their saliva.

Anyone who walks about in a neighbourhood where wasps are common knows what the entrance to a nest looks like: about the size of a mousehole, hidden in the grass or undergrowth, and woe to the casual trespasser. Its guards are as watchful and well-armed as those of the bee colony.

It is an erroneous but widely-held belief that these under-ground nests are different from the hanging sort. The wasp hole we see is only the entrance to a winding passage leading to a cave, from the roof of which hangs the usual nest, well out of the way of any rain water which may accumulate below. Its combs and its covering are just like those of a hanging nest, but it is protected by a layer of soil instead of the roof of a

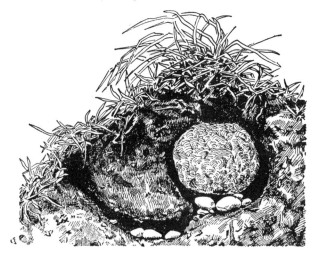

Fig. 57. Underground wasps' nest.

barn. An immense amount of work is involved in the carting away of so many fragments of soil by these small miners. Only the larger pebbles, too heavy even for these diligent beasts, remain lying on the bottom of the cave (fig. 57).

However big a wasps' nest may be—and this is true also of the nest of the hornet which, zoologically speaking, is nothing but a huge wasp—it is the work of a single summer. A colony of ants or bees may continue to exist for many years, or even decades. This is not so with wasps, where each colony in-variably perishes before the end of autumn. The members of a wasp colony do not build up any winter food stores, nor are they able to hibernate like ants. In the autumn they all die, except for a few fertilized females, who manage to hide in a sheltered corner, formed by a layer of moss or a crevice in the rugged bark of a tree, where they outlast the cold season in a state of stupor. In the following spring each of these females will found a colony of her own.

This she does by building a single comb, containing only a few cells at first, which she later surrounds with protecting layers of paper as shown in pl. xxviiia. It is in such a comb that she is to rear her first workers. We are reminded of the way in which ants found their colonies, except that the queen wasp who has to go on providing food for her offspring does not at any time immure herself. Like the queen bee, she deposits each one of her eggs in a separate cell in which the grub develops up to the time of pupating. The first workers, emerging from these pupae, in their turn help the queen with the feeding of the new brood, so that from now on the colony grows with increasing speed. While the first comb is being made wider, another comb is being built beneath it, linked to it by buttresses. The protective cover now has to be enlarged too; new layers being built on top of the old ones which are gradually removed as they become too narrow for the spreading combs. In this way the initial one-comb nest is gradually turned into a large structure made up of several combs arranged one above the other like the different floors in a block of flats. No food is stored in them: they are used only to provide shelter for the rearing of the brood.

However quickly such a colony of wasps may grow, it is unlikely to reach anything like the strength of a large colony of bees or ants, as there will never be more than a few thousand inmates at a time, even in a fair-sized nest. Towards the height of summer the individuals reared in the colony develop into males and into normal females requiring fertilization. While the original queen, as well as those workers and males who live to see the autumn, all perish during the first spell of frost, the young queens, after having been fertilized, go into hiding in good time to guarantee the survival of the tribe into the next year.

In outer appearance and mode of colony-formation, wasps are fairly similar to honey-bees. However, they differ from those flower-loving beings in that, to some extent like ants, they get their food by robbing and murdering their fellow creatures. It is true that they enjoy an occasional meal of sugar or nectar if this is easily accessible. However, their main food, and more particularly that of their young, consists of other insects.

No one who has watched a wasp pouncing on a fly, killing it with one sting, then severing its wings and legs with a few sharp bites of its powerful jaws, and chewing up the remains into pulp, turning an active insect in the twinkling of an eye into a pill brought home as booty; or who has seen a wasp fall upon a bee, her equal in strength and armament, overpowering it and tearing it into pieces to be carried home separately—will be surprised to find, during a summer in which wasps are plentiful, that other insect fauna decline or even die out.

The bumble-bee community

After this short digression on ants and wasps, we are now going to deal with the life of the bumble-bee, which means a return to the main topic of our book. Bumble-bees, in spite of their clumsier appearance, have so much in common with bees, in externals, as well as in internal bodily structure, that zoologists rate them not only as members of the same family but, in fact, their closest relatives.

Inside a dense cushion of moss close to the edge of a wood; beneath the tangled roots of a tree; among tufts of grass growing right in the middle of a meadow; in a deserted mousehole; beneath the floorboards of a wooden shed; these are the sort of places in which we may expect to find the bumble-bee's nest. A comb the size of a man's palm, slovenly built, sheathed in either a waxen envelope or some other cover like a loose wrapper of moss, inhabited by a community of a few dozen, or at the very most, a few hundred inmates—such is the home of the bumble-bee (pl. xxviiib). Flying from flower to flower they feed only on nectar and pollen, and as pollinators only the honey-bee is their superior. Like them, they have a long sucking tongue, pollen baskets, and pollen combs. They also build combs with wax which they themselves exude. The main differences are that while the honey-bee community is perennial the bumble-bee's is annual, and its combs are built in a simpler way. Like wasps they cannot last out the winter, the only survivors being, again, a few fertilized females who are to found the new colonies in the coming spring.

In early spring we can watch those big fat humble-bees, some exploring the ground in all directions, some busying themselves among flowers. These are the queens who, after hibernating, are now in search of a suitable site for their nest, or having found that, are already bringing in the first food stores. At this early period of her life the queen bumble-bee depends entirely on her own resources. In fact, she is as capable as a young queen ant, or queen wasp for that matter, to carry on all the activities which are essential for the survival of the species. In this respect she differs from the queen bee who is not likely to be called upon to perform any of these duties and accordingly seems to have forgotten how to do anything but lay eggs.

The queen bumble-bee builds a small nest, closed on all sides except for the one entrance hole through which the insects slip in and out. She next makes some globular cells inside this nest which are to contain her first brood, and beside them a so-called "honey-pot", a vessel in the form of a big-bellied bottle in which to store the honey that has to serve as food during a period of cold and rainy weather (pl. XXVIIIC). Her building material is a mixture of the wax which she herself has exuded, with resin collected from trees, and pollen from flowers; the habit of using pure wax for building being unknown to the tribe of bumble-bees.

Into the first of these cells the queen deposits some half dozen eggs which she provides with a store of honey and pollen. Then she seals the cell, to open it again at some later occasion in order to bring in another helping of food for her

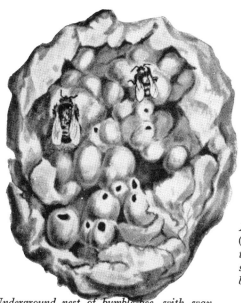

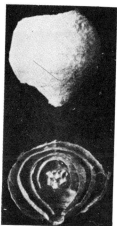

(*a*) *Wasp's nest in early stage; in the middle is the first, single comb, surrounded by protective layers, beneath is the entrance hole*

(*b*) *Underground nest of bumble-bee, with wax covering partly removed to expose the comb. Left, queen; right, worker. About two-thirds life size (after Buttel-Reepen)*

(*c*) *Nest of bumble-bee in early stage. Covering of moss cut and folded back. It is entirely enclosed except for the entrance hole. The queen is still on her own. The first workers will be hatched out in the little comb. On the left is the 'honey-pot'. Life size*

growing larvae. Generally speaking these first of her offspring have to put up with a limited space and scanty food, so
that their growth is stunted. After some time, each of the
larvae starts spinning a cocoon of its own in which to pupate.
Their thrifty mother thereupon gnaws away the cell which
had contained them, so that the pupae are now exposed inside
the nest, as she wants to use for some other purpose the
material that is no longer needed for their protection. The
bumble-bees emerging from these first cocoons are consequently small, with their ovaries incompletely developed
owing to the meagre food supply doled out to them during
their period of growth. They become the first workers,
destined to help the queen build the cells and bring in the food
—tasks which later devolve on them alone so as to enable the
queen to devote all her time to egg-laying. The comb is now
enlarged: it must be said, however, that bumble-bees display
none of the artistic skill that is so characteristic of both wasps
and honey-bees in adding new cells. Theirs are simple
spherical structures built with a primitive waste of space and
material, each cell still having to accommodate several grubs.
The empty cocoons from which workers have emerged serve
later as honey-pots. As the size of the colony grows, the
workers become so numerous that each new brood is better
fed than the last, and brought up in more spacious cradles.
Consequently the adult bumble-bees gradually increase in
size and reach a higher degree of development. In this way,
the bumble-bees produced during the course of a single spring
and summer show all transitional stages, from the first stunted
starvelings to fully-developed females (pl. xxixa). During the
summer, males are also bred who, though not sharing in the
domestic chores, at least are not so dependent on others as
drones: they fly about among the flowers, busy collecting their
own food. Soon they start looking for the young females,
which come flying out of the nest, and fertilization takes place
on the wing. Towards the end of autumn the males perish, as
do the old queen and the whole caste of workers. This is
inevitable, as their food stores, just sufficient for a short

interval of bad weather, cannot tide them over a long winter, nor could their loosely constructed nest protect them against a spell of frost. It is the fertilized females who, after spending the winter in a suitable hiding place, wake up to become the queens of the following year.

CHAPTER SIXTEEN

Solitary Bees and how the Colony began

THE idea that all forms of life on earth today were created together at the beginning of the world was abandoned some time ago, when scientists found out that animals of comparatively simple structure have, in gradual transition, developed into more and more highly organized forms. What is more, even within the short span of our own life, we can watch this process gradually taking place.

Like other existing animals and insects, the community of bees must have reached its present high degree of organization at some definite period in the past. But we have no idea how things happened; nor do we know anything about the ancestors of our present-day bees; they no longer exist and our curiosity about their earthly appearance will probably never be satisfied. However, it is interesting to consider how a community like that of the bumble-bee, which shows a much simpler organization than that of the honey-bee, in spite of the close relation between the two species, may actually represent a stage in its development. For example, the bumble-bees already make some use of their wax secretions in building nests, but they have not reached the stage of building pure wax combs like the honey-bees. Again, although they have learnt how to build cells for accommodating their grubs, they have not yet discovered the most economical way of doing so. Consequently, their building material is quickly exhausted and, as a result, numbers of grubs have to be herded together in each of the narrow cells, a state of affairs which leads to the production of those females with stunted ovaries generally known as workers. Though possessing the feminine instinct for tending and nursing their brood, they have lost all capacity for egg laying. We may well imagine that the first workers ever to appear inside an insect community owed their existence to very similar circumstances.

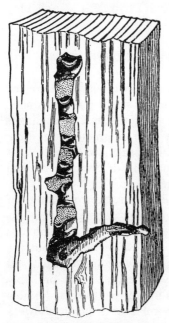

Furthermore, like the honey-bee, the bumble-bees instinctively collect honey and pollen for storage, but their stores do not last them through the winter, so that a female that survives until the following spring will then have to lay and tend her eggs entirely on her own.

Among the members of the bee tribe proper, we encounter forms that show the first signs of social life, alongside with others that are completely lacking in social instinct. It will surprise most readers to learn that the community life seems to be the exception rather than the rule even within the bee family: as many as several thousands of species are known to lead a solitary life. They, also, collect honey and pollen

Fig. 58. Nest of Carpenter Bee with the oldest and biggest grub at the blind end of the hole. (Life size.)

for their brood, and can build cells to house their own grubs; but each female toils for herself and her own particular brood alone with no worker-bees to help her. Each one of these insects strictly obeys a law of nature, but the law which governs the way it has to tend its brood varies greatly from species to species. It is this variety in the behaviour of the solitary bee that makes its history such fascinating reading.

For example, there is one kind of bee (fig. 58) that makes her home in a passage she has bored through a piece of timber.

To the end of this tunnel she carries nectar and pollen which she then forms into a cake, on top of which she lays her egg. Then, retreating far enough to leave space and air for the growing up of the young grub, she erects a protective partition out of little resin balls. A second, third, and fourth chamber are now added, each complete with honey-cake, egg,

Fig. 59. Leaf Cutter Bee at work. (a) *cutting out portions of leaf and flying away with them.* (b) *a finished "thimble" cut out of an oval-shaped piece of leaf (life size).*

and partitioning wall. Finally, she closes the entrance with one last layer of resin, and then leaves her offspring for good. Each grub in turn, as it hatches, finds at its disposal exactly the amount of honey-cake that it needs to complete its own development, after which it pupates inside its little nest of timber and resin. Having emerged from its pupa as a fully-developed bee, it will burrow a passage out into the open. After emerging, males and females meet and mate on the wing; the males soon die, and each of the fertilized females builds a cradle for her future offspring, led by the same instinct that had induced her mother to do so before her, though she herself has never seen her mother performing this feat, and probably will never set eyes on her own offspring.

Or there is the leaf-cutter bee. After scraping out a passage in a piece of rotting timber she will fly to some green bush such as lilac, rose, or raspberry, or perhaps even to a tree like birch or apple, and cut an oval piece out of one of its leaves with the help of her scissor-sharp mandibles. This piece, folded up into a little roll, she carries to her little timber tunnel. Having repeated this performance several times, she rolls the various fragments into one, to form the thimble which is to serve as cradle for her future offspring (fig. 59). You may often have come across these peculiar leaf-cuttings of hers without the least idea of what had made them. The bee puts her honey-cake into the completed thimble and after depositing one egg on top of it she blocks the entrance with a few more of those circular leaf-cuttings.

One of the most perfect nests of all is the nest of one of the mason-bees. For each separate egg—and there are very many of them—she provides one empty snail shell (fig. 60). She puts the food cake right in the middle, and lays her egg on it. At some distance from the centre she separates off a little private chamber, with a partitioning wall made of chewed leaves which have set hard. The space outside this chamber she will fill up with small bits of stone which are prevented from falling out by yet another wall of leaf-pulp. And as if all this was not yet sufficient to protect her offspring against

*XXIX (a) Stages of development of the bumble-bee, from the same nest
(2.ix.35). Next to the fully grown female—the next year's queen—
will be found the still dwarfish workers dating from the beginning of
the nest. Life size*

(b) The snailshell nest, camouflaged with bits of stalk

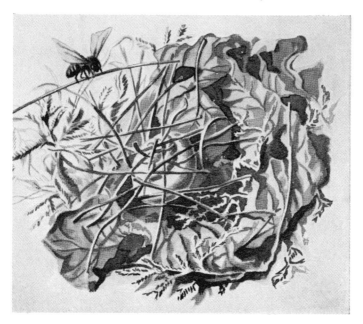

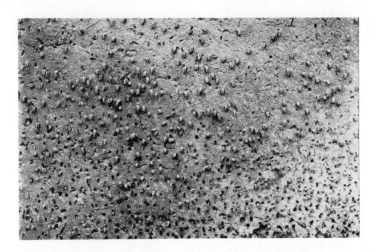

XXX (a) *Colony of mason bees* (anthophora) *in the wall of a house*

(b) *and* (c) *Close-up of part of the wall. The entrance holes to the nest can be seen where the front parts of the tunnels have fallen off*

the manifold dangers that may threaten it from its numerous enemies, she flies untiringly to and fro to gather blade after blade of dry grass—or in some districts pieces of dry twigs or of pine needles—in order to erect a tent-shaped roof under which the snail shell completely disappears (pl. xxixb). One could continue indefinitely in this vein; but it is more interesting to look at the species which show the first recognizable signs of forming some kind of colony.

Once, while travelling in Mecklenburg, I noticed a cow-shed with mud walls that looked as if they had been perforated with shotholes. Actually they were the entrances to the nests of the mason bee, *Anthophora*. Each one had tunnelled into the clay and provided for her brood just as solitary bees do. The bits of clay excavated she had formed into little lumps, out of which she had built a funnel-like entrance passage hanging down from the hole, leading to the main tunnel (pl. xxxa). This is a

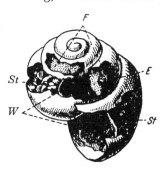

Fig. 60. *Mason Bee's nest in an empty snailshell. F, food. E, egg. W, wall of leaf pulp. St, pieces of stone (twice life size).*

highly temporary structure, liable to be washed away by heavy rain, and of doubtful value to the insect. The interesting point is the existence of this great number of bees in such a limited space. But one finds that this is due not to the sudden emergence of a social instinct but rather to the highly favourable conditions of this particular kind of site. In spite of the proximity, each bee builds for itself and takes no notice of its neighbours. However, this attitude is modified if the whole colony is threatened. Then the bees act together. Many independent observers have noticed that these bees, which are harmless when nesting singly or in small groups, will, when nesting in large groups, attack an intruder as a single swarm.

Such behaviour reveals the existence of a certain social

instinct, which is entirely lacking in most insects, but traces of which are occasionally found among solitary bees. In some species large numbers will hibernate together in a hole specially dug in the ground, or some other cavity. Though external conditions may be the favouring cause for such gathering of insects together, their reaction to such conditions proves the existence of a certain herd instinct, which may be a basic factor in the development of an insect colony.

In its rudimentary form such a herd instinct is found in cases where there is a tendency for insects to gather in groups for no obvious motive or purpose. Figure 61 shows the tip of a withered flower stalk on which several males of a particular species of solitary bee have gathered simply to spend the night together. During the day, in fine weather, they will scatter in all directions, but as soon as it rains or begins to get dark they generally come back to this stalk, or even the very same part of it as before, to take their rest together. Nothing distinguishes their perch from any other in the neighbourhood, yet they invariably return to it. Nor does it offer any special protection from wet or cold. Any flower would fulfil such functions better. Nor do they find any food on it. The one attraction would appear to be the companionship of their own kind.

Fig. 61. Male bees clinging to a dry stalk (life size).

It is a long way from this behaviour to the formation of an insect community. Nevertheless it is possible to imagine that a similar social instinct, if present in females as well as males, and if extended to feeding the brood, may, at some time or other, have led to the formation of a colony. For example, we know one species of bee which tunnels through the mud and widens out a hollow in which she builds a vertical clay comb with several cells (pl. xxxb). She lays an egg in each of these and provides it with a honey cake. But instead of flying off for good after laying her last egg, she will guard her nest until all her brood has emerged. It must be some form of community feeling that makes her offspring stay on in the maternal nest; for they continue together to complete the building of the comb, they all lay their eggs in the common nest, and jointly look after the brood, without building any barriers between their separate families. Food is brought for the whole colony, not for individual offspring. Not until autumn does the colony finally disintegrate, each separate mother proceeding to start a new community in the following spring. What has come into being may be termed a miniature colony.

It is a far cry from such a simple community—via the stricter discipline of the bumble-bees—to the wonderful organization of the honey-bee colony. Nature has unlimited time in which to travel along tortuous paths to an unknown destination. The mind of man is too feeble to discern whence or whither the path runs and has to be content if it can discern only portions of the track, however small.

Index

Age of bees, 39
Antennae of moths, 52, 53
Ants, community of, 160ff.; orientation of, 93
Apiary, 1, 2, 90
Attraction by scent, 52, 115

Beehive, 4ff.
Bee louse, 155
Bee wolf, 153
Body, appearance of, 2; and retention of scent, 12; temperature, 23ff.
Brood, 19ff.; care of, 23, 24, 36; comb, 20ff.; nurses, 37
Bumble-bees, 169ff.
Butterflies, sensitivity of taste, 61; colour vision, 70

Campanula, 127ff.
Camphor, 57
Caterpillars, 11, 22
Cells, shape of, 7, 135ff.
Clothes moths, 156
Clouds, 96
Clover, 10, 11, 13, 68, 135
Colour, blindness, 64ff.; and butterflies, 70; and flowers, 67ff.; memory for, 149; of hives, 87ff.; and scent, 49ff.; training to, 65ff.
Comb, 6ff., 20ff.; movable, 5; of wasps' nest, 166
Communication, 100–36
Crystalline cone, 75, 84
Cyclamen, 106ff., 110ff.

Dance, round, 101ff.; connection with abundance of supply, 112; on a flat surface, 121ff.; of pollen collectors, 118, 126ff.; in the swarm cluster, 132ff.; the wagging, 116ff.
Dark room, training to time in, 141
Digger wasp, 153
Direction-finding, 85ff., 121ff. See also Orientation

Egg-laying, 3, 19ff.; of bumble-bees,

170; of solitary bees, 173ff.
Egypt, bees in ancient, 4
Essential oils, 48, 49
Eye, 2, 63–84; and colour, 64–71; structure of, 71–7; visual acuity of, 77ff.; and shapes, 77ff.; and polarized light, 81ff. See also Colour

Faceted eye, 75ff.
Fan experiment, 124
Feelers, 55ff. See Antennae
Fertilization of bees, 25, 29, 31; of flowers by bees, 17, 45, 135
Filters, light, see Polarized light
Flea, 9
Flight, orientation, 37, 85ff., 96; queen's, 25, 28, 31, 90; range of, 118
Flower, colours, 67ff.; constancy, 45; scent, 45ff., 106ff., 127, 135. See also Honey, Pollen
Foul brood, 159

Glands, changes in, 37ff.; scent, 115
Glow-worm's eye, 77
Gravity, use of, in wagging dance, 122ff., 129
Greenfly, 163; as wax producer, 6

Hearing, 29
Hexagonal cells, 7
Hive, 4ff.; colour of, 87ff.; observation, 20, 34, 41; hinged observation, 129 ff.
Honey, 10ff., 61, 63; as food, 13, 152; stomach, 12
Humming birds, 69

Insect-pollinated plants, 68
Intelligence, 149

Language of bees, 100ff.
Larvae, 22ff.; of ants, 162, 165; of bumble-bees, 170
Learning ability, 45ff., 60, 63, 85ff., 96, 107ff., 138ff., 150

181